DON'T KNOW WHERE W...
IN NO HURRY TO GET...
AND STILL ARRIVING...

A CHRONOLOGICAL HISTORY OF

KEY WEST

A TROPICAL ISLAND CITY

STEPHEN NICHOLS

PUBLISHED in the UNITED STATES by:
KEY WEST IMAGES OF THE PAST, INC.
P.O. Box 1237
Key West, FL 33041
(305) 294-4142
-- In association with --
OLD TOWN TROLLEY TOURS®
1910 N. Roosevelt Boulevard
Key West, FL USA 33040

Book Design: Stephen Nichols

PHOTO CREDITS:
Monroe County Library, Processing by Adolph Gucinski: 1838, 58, 71, 92 &
    1904, 07, 08, 12 (both), 14, 19, 22, 24, 27, 35, 41, 49, 55, 69, 79, 80, 94.
Edwin O. Swift, Jr.: Front & back covers, 1849 & 1905, 46, 56,
    69 (of shark), 71, 81, 87
Edwin O. Swift, III: 1975 (both)
Wendy Tucker: 1978
Wright Langley: 1983
Treasure Salvors, Inc.: 1985
Richard Watherwax: 1989
Alex Vega : 1995

ILLUSTRATION CREDITS:
C. Buckholz: Late 1700's & 1825, 37, 77, 85 & 1921, 34, 67, 72
R. Lee: Title Page, 1832, 82 & 1931, 49
From the collection of W. Langley: 1910
R. E. Kennedy: 1990
Other: S. Nichols

ABOUT THE AUTHOR:
    Stephen Nichols moved to Key West in 1983. He was the Director
    of the Restoration of Old City Hall in Key West from 1986 until
    1990, then a bellman at the Casa Marina 'til 1995 and now legally
    represents Livingston Dickinson, the only Jack Russell Terrior in
    the U.S. not working in film or commercials.

DEDICATION

To Dr. Ross McElwee, a passionate student of life and
a thoroughgoing gentleman.
And (1996) to Jeannie Faye Jasim, my best friend.

THANKS TO:
Wright & Joan Langley
Jenny Lee Quinnell & Sharon Wells
Ed Swift, Piper Smith, Sue Barroso & Barry Barroso
Tom Hambright, Sylvia Knight, Allan Merrill, Linda Sorensen,
Bill Wright, Melvin & Patty Cohen, Wendy Tucker,
Emelia Fernandez (The Cuban Coffee Queen), Bernie Papy, Jr.,
Sharon French, Jack Hamm ...

SECOND EDITION:
Mike Best, "T.P." Jim Kruschke, John & Ann Dickinson,
Capt. Steve & "T.B." Dianne Allerton, Suzanne McCaughey,
Felix & Virginia Cooper, Cynthia Gooch Copley,
J.T. Thompson & Solares Hill Design Group.

SECOND EDITION ADDENDUM:
Typos in the first edition have been pretty much corrected and some
additional copy added for clarification. The second edition continues from
1988 thru 1995 with new text, photos and illustrations.

THIRD EDITION ADDENDUM:
The Third Edition continues from 1996 thru 2000.

Old Town Trolley welcomes you to the southernmost city in the continental United States ... the edge of America.

The original trolley system began its run in 1885 as a mule drawn streetcar transporting our city's cigar workers to the factories. By the turn of the century, these trolleys converted to electric streetcars carrying both locals and visitors around one of Florida's largest metropolitan cities ... Key West, Florida. After World War I, the trolleys began to deteriorate and by 1926, the system was discontinued.

In 1980, Old Town Trolley Tours began with a fleet of authentically styled vehicles designed after those that traversed our island at the turn of the century. Nowadays the trolley conductors present a fully narrated tour of Key West coupled with the conveniences of on and off boarding privileges which permit individual sightseeing, dining and shopping.

This book is the perfect companion to our tour in that it highlights the island's unique history, eclectic characters and stages of development. It was produced in response to the many requests of our guests who couldn't remember the wealth of information heaped upon them by ... no, wait a minute ...

Actually, this book was created to accurately portray the myriad aspects of the history of Key West. History is story-telling; a phase of life that we all should, and, if you think about it, we all do enjoy. That's why we, at Old Town Trolley, are delighted to say, "Don't just visit Key West, Relive it!" Have a great time!

INTRODUCTION

As the southernmost point in the continental United States, the island of Key West is bordered by the Straits of Florida and the Gulf of Mexico.

The island is 1.25 miles wide and almost 4 miles long, comprising 2,752 acres. It is located at the end of the Florida Keys and lies 155 miles south of Miami, 98 miles north of Havana and the Tropic of Cancer; on a latitudinal scale, Key West is 375 miles south of Cairo, Egypt. Highway U.S. 1 begins in Key West and ends, after 2,209 miles, in Fort Kent, Maine.

The frost-free weather, swept by tradewinds, is south Florida's warmest in winter and coolest in summer.
Average daily temperature: 79°F
Highest recorded temperature: 97°F (1886)
Lowest recorded temperature: 41°F (1981)
Average yearly rainfall: 39.9 inches

Evolving on a coral limestone base, the highest point on the isle is 18 feet above mean sea level and is called Solares Hill. With a natural deep water channel harbor (20 feet plus), entered by way of the Northwest Channel that cuts through the only living coral reef in the continental U.S., Key West provides the mariner protection from weather, fog and war.

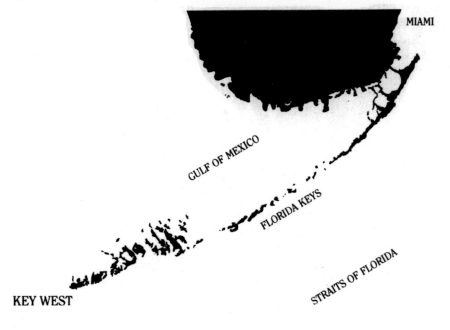

MIAMI

GULF OF MEXICO

FLORIDA KEYS

STRAITS OF FLORIDA

KEY WEST

CUBA

DUVAL STREET, KEY WEST, LOOKING WEST

PHOTO BY ED SWIFT, JR.

The Sargasso Sea is a calm, equatorial body of water in the Atlantic, choked with floating seaweed, inhabited by scampering crabs and baked by the tropical sun. To the west of it travels the South Equatorial Current which passes the eastern coast of Brazil and heads north to the Caribbean Sea and around the western tip of Cuba. At that point, it carroms off the entrapped waters of the Gulf of Mexico and is injected into the Straits of Florida. The current moves at 4 to 5 knots and transports a water load 50 times greater than all of the major rivers of the worlds combined, moving somewhere in the neighborhood of 75,000,000 tons of water every second. It is a river in the ocean and the pressure of its surge raises the water level almost 7 inches.

Benjamin Franklin named this river the Gulf Stream, a continuous band of warm water that passes within 7 to 12 miles of Key West, then heads up the east coast of the United States, passes Bermuda, crosses the Atlantic and deposits a thermal climate on Western Europe.

But back in the days of Columbus, they didn't know what it was. You could be sailing along with the prevailing westerlies and pieces of ocean debris would overtake your ship and pass on by. If you were proceeding against the current with the wind aft, you could sail all day with full sails and make no headway. It was a mystery, this river in the ocean. However, in the area of the Tropic of Cancer, the weather was very pleasant, migrating sea animals were everywhere, there were plenty of birds around and exotic islands kept poking up from the depths. It was an interesting place to explore.

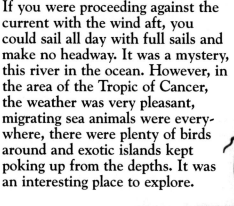

1513

Ponce de Leon, on his voyage of the Indies, discovers Key West and establishes Spanish claim to the island. During that time period, Key West was inhabited by Calusa Indians who had been driven all the way south in wars with the Tequesta Indians of southern Florida. When the Spanish landed, they found Indian bones (from the wars) lying on the ground and in the trees of the island. The Indians, either for religious or topographic (the ground is very, very hard) reasons, did not bury their dead.

The name Key West is derived from the Spanish "Cayo Hueso," which translates into "Bone Key," and was phonetically engineered by the English into "Key West."

There is evidence that John & Sebastian Cabot sailed past Key West as early as 1497. While Ponce de Leon never set foot on Key West, he did officially claim it for Spain.

Early 1700's

The Calusa Indians, who were mariners and fishermen, were finally driven out of Key West by the Seminoles and escaped to Cuba in ocean-going canoes.

A few Spaniards joined the remaining Indians and settled Key West.

1763

England had captured Havana; Spain trades Florida for Cuba.

1783

With the English unable to maintain a strong settlement, Spain reclaims Key West.

Late 1700's

Key West, with its strategic location near Havana and at the split of shipping lanes between New Orleans, at the mouth of the Mississippi River, and the United States' east coast, becomes a pirate's paradise.

Piracy had long been big business in the Caribbean beginning with Sir Walter Raleigh's ships preying on Spanish galleons in the 1600's. Among the more notorious and famous pirates (fraternal name: "The Brethren of the Coast") operating in the area were Captain Teach (Blackbeard), Captain Kidd and Captain Black Ceasar.

1815

Don Juan de Estrada, the Spanish governor of Florida, grants the deed to Key West to one Juan P. Salas (Royal Artillery Corps, St. Augustine) for "unspecified" military services. Salas, who is traveling the Caribbean, does nothing with Key West.

1819

United States establishes a territorial government in part of Florida. Salas becomes nervous.

1820

Ellen Mallory, first Anglo white woman settler, arrives in Key West, is widowed and opens the first boarding house. She is the mother of Stephen Mallory, who is to serve in the Confederate cabinet of Jefferson Davis during the Civil War.

1821

Florida's first land fraud (maybe).

While in a Havana bar, Juan P. Salas, fearing the U.S. occupation of Florida, sells Cayo Hueso to John W. Simonton of Mobile. Simonton, eager to make everything official with all of the U.S./Spanish/English paperwork floating around about Key West, goes to Washington and encounters General John Geddes of South Carolina, who also owns Key West which he bought from one John Strong who had also previously purchased Cayo Hueso from Juan P. Salas.

Spain cedes its part of Florida territory to the U.S. and Andrew Jackson is appointed as the first U.S. military governor.

Simonton's Washington influences are better than Geddes'.

1822

U.S. Congress consolidates East and West Florida into the Territory of Florida. William P. Duval is first civilian territorial governor.

Simonton takes possession of Key West which is declared a U.S. Port of Entry. First customs house opens.

Lt. M.C. Perry, commander of the U.S. Schooner *Shark,* is ordered to visit and explore Key West. Perry, an opportunist, renames Key West as "Thompson's Island," after the Secretary of the Navy.

Key West (formerly Cayo Hueso, Bone Key, Thompson's Island) is then renamed "Allentown" (why not?), but mapmakers can't keep up. Key West emerges as the official name.

1823-1824

With heavy sea traffic from Havana, various government and private vessels establish the Key West port and naval depot.

Pirates have a field day!

The U.S. government budgets $160,000 and sends Commodore David Porter to clean up the waters off of Key West.

Fortifications are begun, the U.S. Marines are established and the "Mosquito Fleet" of the West Indies Anti-Piracy Squadron begins to annihilate the pirates.

Meanwhile, the real mosquito fleet spreads yellow fever ("They're worse than the pirates," said Porter) and 40% of the enlisted men die.

1825-1827

When regular seagoing traffic sailing the Straits of Florida wasn't caught between the pirates and Commodore Porter, the ships were washing up on the reef just off Key West.

"Wreck on the reef!" was the cry that launched a furious race to sea by Key West wreckers. The first captain on board his ship to reach the doomed wreck was designated as wrecking master.

The crew and passengers were saved and many settled in Key West. The cargoes of silks, laces, satins, leather, hides, lumber, silver, china and crystal, tobacco, furniture, fine wines, whiskey, rum and everything else (rigging, windows, stoves, etc.) became the property of the captain and crew.

Wrecking became a major economic influence on Key West. When not wrecking, the crews fished.

U.S. Congress (1825) enacts law outlawing the salvaging of wrecks in American waters by any other than American vessels. Population of American-owned ships skyrockets.

167 ships, surviving reefs, enter Key West harbor (1826). First lighthouse built.

Population of Key West (1827) passes 300.

1828

Monroe County (named for the president) is established.

The Supreme Court for the Southern Judicial District of the Territory of Florida is called to order. James Webb (Georgia) is the first judge. First lawyers arrive.

"Island of Key West" is incorporated, then changed and incorporated as "Town of Key West," then (1832) changed and incorporated as "City of Key West."

1829

The Post Office is established, mail is delivered monthly by the 10-ton *Post Boy* sailing from Charleston. The small sailing vessel usually arrives every six weeks.

The oldest surviving house in Key West is built by ship carpenters for Richard Cussans from Nassau. It was later deeded to Captain Frances Watlington, a successful Key West wrecker. The house is now known as "The Wreckers Museum" and is located at 322 Duval Street.

1830

Richard Fitzpatrick starts the first salt manufacturing business, proclaiming salt as the "most probable means of making the place (Key West) known to the commercial world." Salt is used as a preservative and as money.

The salt is to be manufactured by flooding flat ponds through a series of dikes; as the tide goes out, the salt water evaporates leaving salt crystals up to one-quarter inch in size. If it happened to rain, however, the crop would dissolve.

Fitzpatrick went out of business in 1834. He was followed by a series of other investing consorts until the 1850's when, with acquired knowledge and slave labor, W.C. Dennis shipped 75,000 bushels on 500 ships. Most of the salt was sold to fish houses in the Carolinas and Virginia.

Salt was big business until the Civil War when salt gathering was suspended in Key West (a Union town) so as to not bolster the economic scenario of the Confederacy (rest of the South).

The hurricane of 1876 destroyed the salt ponds and the business died.

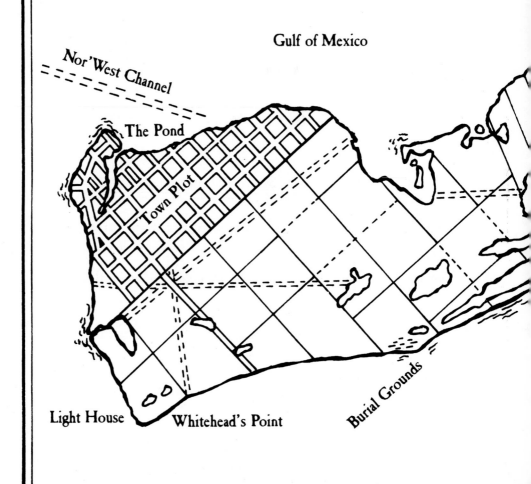

The Island of Key West
by Wm. A. Whitehead

Gulf of Mexico

Nor'West Channel

The Pond

Town Plot

Light House

Whitehead's Point

Burial Grounds

1831

Key West population: 360
Deaths: 14
Mayoral votes: 39
Number of buildings: 81

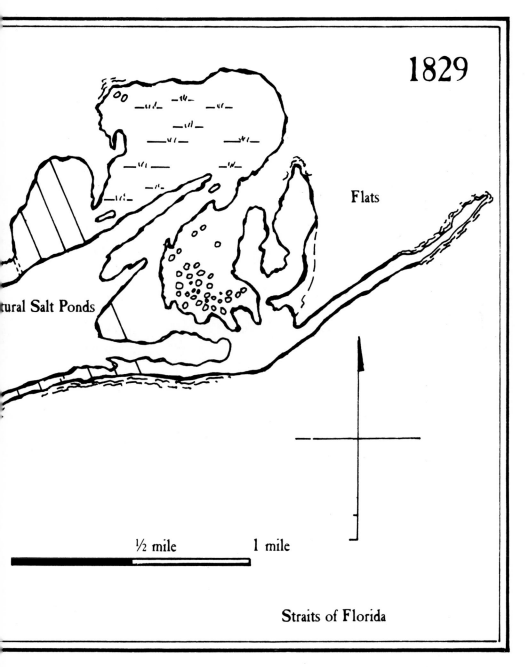

1829

Flats

tural Salt Ponds

½ mile   1 mile

Straits of Florida

Property Value: $65,923
Taxes paid: $1,300
Ships harbored: 303
Import/Export value: $172,721
Customs House revenues: $45,000
    William H. Wall, a shipwrecked Englishman, starts first cigar
factory employing 50 Cubans using primo Cuban tobacco.

1832

Ornithologist John James Audubon visits Key West while working on his natural history album, *"Birds of America."* He stays at the home of Captain John Geiger.

Audubon House—Key West   R LEE '79

1833

Key West is the richest city per capita in the South.

1834

First school opened by the Reverend Alvah Bennett of St. Paul's Protestant Episcopal Church.

St. Paul's, the oldest church in south Florida, was started in 1832, the first church built in 1840; destroyed by an 1846 hurricane; rebuilt; destroyed by THE 1886 fire; rebuilt; destroyed by a 1909 hurricane. The present building has survived since 1912.

1835

Halley's Comet passes and first recorded hurricane hits Key West. Fortunately, St. Paul's is not yet built.

1836

First fire company starts with Joseph A Thouron as foreman and 25 volunteers. First fire engine bought. When (1843) Browne's warehouse burns, the engine fails to pump and frustrated firemen push it off a pier.

1837

Estava and Williams cigar factory opens and Key West's cigar dynasty begins to expand.

The "smokers" are made from very high quality Cuban tobacco which is graded by color (golden) and color consistency. The wrapper (best leaf) is rolled over the filler which is of a lesser grade due to the color consistency.

Spain began putting heavy tariffs on Cuban tobacco and economically discontented cigar barons began to move to Key West.

1869: Vincente Ybor moves to Key West and establishes factories.

1873: 4,000 Cubans immigrate.

1875: Key West is the largest cigar manufacturing center.

1876: Key West's largest cigar manufacturers are:
"La Rosa Española" (Seidenburg) employs 600
"Principe de Gales" (Ybor) employs 400

1879: First cigar maker's union begins and that doesn't sit well
with owners who had left Cuba to get away from unions.
Trouble continues between Cubans and Spaniards
(loyal to Spain's dominance of Cuba) as owners treat
illegally imported Spaniards better.
1886: Tampa initiates campaign to lure cigar industry, offering
low taxes, few labor problems and swampland for
building. Welcome to Tampa, Ybor leaves Key West.
1888: 200 factories; 6,000 men; 100,000,000 handrolled cigars
and then business begins to decline.
1931: Last large cigar factory closes.

There is a strong correlation between the cigar industry
and Cuba's struggle for independence from Spain as money,
discontented Cuban refugees and revolutionary idealisms began
to focus in Key West.

BUSINESS DISTRICT, KEY WEST, 1838

1838

City prohibits filling of tidal pool known as "The Pond"
(currently under the site of Old City hall) by encroaching
business district. Landowners are forced to keep their submerged
property submerged to allow the tides to keep the water moving
and prevent the swarming of malaria-carrying mosquitoes.

1846: Hurricane washes sand into the pond and hinders tidal flow.
1853: Landowners are now required to fill by the City.
1871: Simonton's Estate gives parcel to City for City Hall
site on Greene Street.

1839-1841

Wreckers are still doing a gangbuster business. They are,
however, at a complete loss to explain how false channel lights
appear on the reef.

1842

Oldest schoolhouse is built; first private school, called the
Baldwin House.
School taxes are implemented to assist kids unable to pay
for the private school.

1843

Key West has its first big fire that destroys F.A. Browne's warehouse. At this time, Browne, a partner of William Curry, is Key West's most successful marine merchant and wrecker.

General Narcisso Lopez arrives from Cuba to raise the first army to attempt to overthrow Spanish dominance of Cuba. Because of U.S. / Spanish neutrality laws, Lopez is captured by the U.S. and the revolt is temporarily arrested.

1844

The first benevolent society, "Free and Accepted Masons," begins with 8 members.

The U.S. Marine Hospital is built on Emma Street. Designed by Robert Mills, architect of the Washington Monument.

1845

Florida is admitted to the Union.

Ft. Zachary Taylor, a massive naval fortress, is started at the entrance to Key West Harbor. The Navy now regards Key West as "the Gibraltar of the Gulf," a strategic name first suggested by Lt. M.C. Perry in 1822.

1846

BIG HURRICANE!
Ft. Taylor construction is destroyed.
Lighthouse demolished.
$1,600,000 in wreckers' revenues.
Many buildings are severely damaged, totally destroyed or blown away.
Horses and cattle are washed out to sea.
The cemetery, located on South Beach where a hole could be dug, is washed away; many of the coffins are launched out to sea.

1847

Cemetery grounds are purchased at a higher elevation along Angela Street (present site). Some of the deceased are now buried above ground in mausoleums.

Dr. Joseph Porter is born in the mansion at the corner of Duval and Caroline Streets. Dr. Porter, involved in extensive research of yellow fever, helped eliminate the disease by implementing quarantine laws. Patients were first quarantined on ships.
Dr. Porter, later Florida's first Public Health officer, died in 1927 in the same room in which he was born.

1848

Captain John Bartlum's house arrives. Called "the Bahama House" (Eaton and William Streets), it was built with wooden pegs, rather than nails, on Green Turtle Cay in the Bahamas. It was then taken apart, shipped and reassembled in Key West.

1849

New lighthouse is completed further inland. Originally 66 feet tall, it has since been increased to 81 feet for a better sighting. Decommissioned by the Coast Guard in 1962, it now is the Lighthouse Museum.

PHOTO BY ED SWIFT, JR.

1850

The reef is officially marked with lights.

The wrecking business begins to slow down drastically due to lighthouse construction, accurate channel markers and regulations outlawing false beacons. While salvaged goods continued to be auctioned on Saturdays at the custom's warehouse, wrecking slowly fades and, in 1921, wrecking courts were closed forever.

1851

Narcisso Lopez departs Key West to attack Spanish-held Cuba for the second time. Undermanned, underfinanced, unsuccessful.

1852

First Roman Catholic Church is dedicated, "Church of St. Mary, Star of the Sea." St. Paul is Key West's patron saint. The church is destroyed by fire in 1901.

1853

Marine railway dry dock is built (largest vessel accomodated, 519 tons) by William Curry.

The penniless Curry arrived in Key West from the Bahamas in 1837. Curry had since done well in the lucrative wrecking days and opened William Curry's Sons Ship Chandlery and wrecking warehouses; then went on to become a Key West mayor.

When he died in 1896, Curry was reputedly Florida's richest man and first millionaire.

1854-1857

The people who settled Key West are known as Conchs, a loosely defined dynasty that still sort of reigns in Key West.

The wealthiest, with well-kept lineage notes, were of Anglo-Saxon and Celtic stock; their ancestors first settled New England and the South.

When the Revolutionary War broke out, they (being loyal to England) moved to Bermuda, then the Bahamas and Jamaica. After the war and the loss of colony tax income, King George III began taxing his Caribbean territories. The Conchs acknowledged with sincere apologies the error of their ways and moved to Key West, United States of America, as proud American citizens.

Conchs picked up the name due to their varied uses of the tough shellfish for steaks, chowder, fritters and as musical instruments.

This is important: Conch is pronounced "konk."

1858

Ft. Taylor, begun in 1846, is near completion. Emphasis on the Mexican War has slowed contruction for 12 years.

FORT JEFFERSON, MORE BRICKS THAN ANY OTHER STRUCTURE IN THE WESTERN HEMISPHERE.

Construction at Ft. Jefferson, also started in 1846, creeps along. Built 70 miles west of Key West on a very small island in the Dry Tortugas, the fort later became infamous as the prison home of Dr. Samuel Mudd (set John Wilkes Booth's broken leg) who courageously fought a yellow fever epidemic at the fort and was pardoned in 1869. Work finally stopped in 1886 as the fort was now obsolete in its defense capabilities. Ft. Jefferson is now a national monument and the nation's most isolated national park.

1859

Key West has its first gigantic fire (even bigger than the fire of 1843) and the entire waterfront district up to Greene Street burns. For unknown reasons, Key West has no organized fire department or equipment . . . probably one of those "we'll get to it manana" deals. Anyway, the fire more than likely would have burnt up the whole town except for Henry "Hero" Mulrenon.

Mulrenon runs to Ft. Taylor, grabs a keg of gunpowder, runs back to his house (Greene and Fitzpatrick Streets) and blows it up. The sacrifice of his home creates a fire break and the spread of the fire is halted.

1860

A stew of problems begins to boil with the Northern industrial and Southern agrarian states. The majority of Key Westers are mostly sympathetic to the Southern cause.

The largest town meeting in Key West history is called and by an overwhelming vote the local citizens decide that, if the South secedes, Key West is with 'em!

The following day Key West goes Union.

Here's how it happened: U.S. Captain John M. Brannon realizes the strategic importance of the "Gibraltar of the Gulf" and, determined to keep it out of Confederate hands, sneaks his troops that night into the almost-finished-but-on-maintenance status Fort Taylor.

The next day Key West decides to stay Union and continue business as usual.

1861

The Civil War starts, construction is finished on Ft. Taylor and begins on East and West Martello Towers, which are to serve as sidearms and batteries for the fort. When completed, the martellos are connected to Ft. Taylor by railroad tracks for movement of munitions.

U.S. Navy begins blockade of Mississippi/East Coast Confederate shipping with the East Coast Blockade Squadron. Over 200 blockade runners are captured.

Confederate flags begin appearing in Key West. It seems most locals are still sympathetic to the South and irritated with the war effort's disruption of their sponging and cigar businesses.

1862

Caroline Lowe stands on top of her house and waves a large Confederate flag. Though searched many times, the Yankees can never find the "rumored" flag. Later, hiding places are revealed in a stairway banister post and under her hooped skirt.

1863

The Civil War gets out of hand.

Confederate sympathizers are told to get out of town and move within the Rebel lines. The Union will even provide their passage. The confusing situation, with orders now coming from both Union and Confederate armies, was straightened out when U.S. Colonel J.H. Good arrived with the 47th Pennsylvania Regiment and terminated ALL orders.

1864-1866

Key West sees little action for the rest of Civil War.

There is a memorial erected by the Navy Club in honor of Union soldiers stationed in Key West who died of yellow fever. The fence surrounding the monument (at Clinton Place) was built by Confederate veteran J.V. Harris.

1867

Telegraph cable is laid across Straits of Florida by International Ocean Telegraph Company and connects Key West to Cuba.

1868

Carlos Manuel de Cespedes leads the first successful revolutionary movement against Spanish dominance of Cuba. Bloody battles between "Cuba Libres" and loyalist Spaniards spread throughout Cuba.

Migration to Key West picks up as refugees come to the U.S. for political freedoms, economic resources and a better life.

1869

Refugees from Cuba including cigar factory owners and rollers secretly begin to open financial avenues to back the Cuban revolution.

Vicente Ybor flees Cuba and moves his cigar factory to Key West which begins the dominant period of the cigar industry.

1870

General Melchoir Aguerra arrives in Key West to raise funds for the Cuban revolution. Funds are filtered through the cigar industry, now the largest in the world.

1871

San Carlos Institute built, named for Carlos Manuel de Cespedes.

San Carlos served as a Cuban school, Cuban consulate and bilingual theater. The wooden building was destroyed in the 1886

THE SAN CARLOS INSTITUTE,
KEY WEST

fire, rebuilt and blown apart in the 1919 hurricane and then, finally, built with concrete in 1924. It fell into disrepair after Castro's revolution when Cuban diplomatic ties were broken with U.S. San Carlos opens 1/5/92 after a tumultuous and magnificent restoration operation carved up by warring Cuban factions in Miami and Key West over control of the Institute. The building features a magnificent theatre and restored classrooms.

1872

Spanish authorities in Cuba order U.S. to observe neutrality laws and begin trials in Key West of suspected revolutionary arms merchants. Trials are held and all, as luck would have it, end in acquittals.

1873

Mallory Steamship Company commences service to New York and Galveston.

The worldwide shipping company was not created by Stephen Mallory, one of Key West's most illustrious citizens. It was Mallory who argues in 1856 for the establishment of a strategic naval presence on the island. Mallory served as City Marshall, Customs Inspector and Attorney. He was an authority on admiralty and wrecking laws and U.S. Senator for Florida, a position he resigned to become Secretary of the Confederate Navy.

Mallory Steamship Company was started by Clyde Mallory.

1874

Sears School, the city's first public school, is built on Simonton Street. The building was torn down in 1909.

1875

Population: 12,733
Assessed property value: $1,505,720
Taxes paid: City: $11,728 • County: $16,253
State: $19,346 • Federal: $164,870
Four people die of diarrhea.

1876

Crops grown in Key West: Date, Coconut, Lime, Lemon, Grape, Pomegranate, Guava, Sapodilla, Banana, Mango, Citron, Fig, Plum, Sugarcane, Salt, Avocado, Orange, Grapefruit, Jamaican Apple, Soursop, Papaya, Indian Almond and a few Peaches.

1877-1881

The spongers would set out in a large sailing boat towing a number of smaller skiffs. A two-man crew worked each skiff; one to pole or row, the other guiding. The "hooker" would spread shark oil on the surface to calm and clarify the waters. Using a three-pronged hook on a pole, the hooker grabbed the sponge from depths of up to 30 feet.

The first cargo was shipped to New York in 1849 and the $10,000 crop, thought worthless because no one had ever heard of sponges from the U.S., was almost destroyed. At its height, the Key West sponge industry involved 350 boats, 1,800 spongers and a $750,000 annual crop.

Greek spongers arrived in Key West in the late 1800's and employed a new method of harvesting. In diving suits pumped with air, the Greeks simply walked on the ocean floor picking up their harvest. The Greeks also had a tendency to take every sponge they could get their hands on. The local spongers had a tendency to accidently hook the divers' air hoses. The Greeks moved to Tarpon Springs around the turn of the century.

A red tide in 1910 wiped out the Key West sponge beds, the Greeks wiped out the Tarpon Springs sponge beds.

1882-1884

Key West's fanciest house, "The Gingerbread House," is constructed by Benjamin Baker who presents it as a gift to his daughter. The house was blown off its foundation in 1970 by a tornado and had to be lifted back into place.

Residential architecture of this and later periods sets a stage in Key West that reminds visitors of "somewhere else besides Florida," which is exactly what it reminded settling homebuilders of . . . home.

Locals were able to reside in homes they were accustomed to and comfortable in by combining elements of Victorian style with tropical home engineering (wraparound porches, high ceilings with tall windows, hatches in the roof; all incorporated to provide shade while funneling breezes). Construction utilized the available, rugged, termite-resistant Dade County pine.

Ornate gingerbread molding details, captain's walks, exotic woods and everything else salvaged from wrecks, tin roofs, jungles of tropical vegetation, lack of land creating close proximities and a general attitude of building without strict obedience to your neighborhood theme helped to further distinguish the patterns of local architectonics.

1885

The first street railway, powered by mules, is set in motion by Eduardo Gato, one of Key West's wealthiest cigarmakers. The streetcar was used primarily to get his cigar rollers to work.

General Maximo Gomez arrives in Key West to smuggle arms and men back to Cuba for a revolution. By loading men on one ship and guns on another, then meeting out at sea and combining cargoes, Gomez was able to successfullly violate neutrality laws on a technicality.

1886

Key West's most devastating fire erupts in the center of town at San Carlos. Rumored to be deliberately set by Spanish loyalists, the fire quickly burst from the back rooms of the building and spread through the city in two directions.

The fire department was alerted!

Unfortunately, Key West's only fire engine, a steam-powered pumper, happened to be in New York for repairs. The fire

BIRD'S

KEY W

KEY

FLA.

47—J. W. Pierce, Clothing and Gents Furnishings, etc
48—Samuel Filer, Dealer in Lumber, Lath and Shingles.
49—John Lowe, Jr. Groceries and Ship handling
50—Estate of Henry Lowe, General Merchandise
51—Theo. Pinder, Groceries, Provisions, etc
52—Alphous Lowe, Tin, Copper and Sheet Iron Work
53—Louis A. Crouse, Watches, Clocks and Jewelry
54—Geo. W. Martin, Groceries and Bakery
55—J. J. Warren, Watches, Clocks and Jewelry
56—Perry & Curtis Groceries, Merchandise
57—Pent & Navarro, Cigar Manufactories Nos 10, 11 & 21
58—Gideon Lowe, Sr, Dry Goods and Millinery
59—John F. Wescott's Restaurant and Ice Cream Parlor
60—Cayetano Soria's Cigar Manufactories Nos 23 and 24
61—Estate J. P. Roberts, Dry Goods, Groceries and Ship
      Chandlery
62—S. S. Lowe, Dry Goods and Groceries
63—John W. Sawyer, Clothing, Gents Furnishing, Boots and
      Shoes, Hats, Caps, etc
64—J. F. Hanson, General Blacksmithing
65—R. J. Perry, Druggist

61—R. Asbury & Son, General Merchandise
65—John Kemp, Dry Goods, Groceries and Bakery
66—Wm. H. Williams, Groceries, Blacksmithing
67—Richard Curry, Saloon
68—John W. Weatherford, Saloon
69—A. A. Brooks, Livery, Feed and Sale Stable
70—A. J. Harris, General Merchandise
71—H. H. Walton, Dry Goods and Groceries
72—Bro. J. V. Albury, General Merchandise
73—Robert J. Pent, Groceries, Groceries and Notions
74—Philip Thompson, Editor Key West Democrat
75—J. V. Vek, Groceries and Merchant, Steamship Agent and
      Ship Broker, Wharves, Warehouses, Bituminous and
      Anthracite Coals
76—Coleman & Harbor   Groceries and General Commission Merchants
      Edwin Thompson, Manufacturer of Fancy Mottos
      Novel   Dealer   Fine Curtains
      J. P. Kemp, Tailor
      H. M. Hilton   Key West Blanket
      Russell House, Chas. T. Merrill, Manager
      H   Sam, Editor, Key of the Gulf

department, resorting to previous firefighting techniques, blew up
a few buildings. Unfortunately again, sparks from the explosions
drifted onto nearby roofs. The fire took off and burned up the entire
wooden commercial district, wharfs, warehouses and City Hall.

1887

The first Jewish synagogue is organized as new arrivals settle
and open up shops.

1888

Business is great! Sponging, cigarmaking, salvage and wrecking,
fishing, mercantilism, and the military make Key West a happy town.

1889

Key West is the largest and wealthiest city in Florida.

1890

The Monroe County Courthouse (Whitehead Street) is completed.
Artificial ice plant begins operation; Green Parrot Bar (formerly
the Brown Derby) opens.
The Little White House is built. Originally designed as the
home of the Navy's Commandant and Paymaster, "Quarters
A & B" soon evolved into the base V.I.P. Quarters. While
Presidents Taft, Coolidge, Franklin Roosevelt, Truman,
Eisenhower and Kennedy all visited Key West, only Truman
actually stayed overnight in the building.
Originally, the Little White House sat on oceanfront property
that was filled in 1938 to provide space for the Administration
Building during World War II.

1891

Construction booms in Key West. The Post Office and Customs
House (a midwestern design with fireplaces and high sloping roofs
designed to prevent snow accumulation), First National Bank
(built by Cuban cigar manufacturers) and City Hall are completed.
Old City Hall was designed by William Kerr, an Irishman and
a very popular local architect. The Romanesque Revival building
featured 16-foot ceilings on two floors with a grand two-story cast
iron stairway entrance. The second floor served as city commission
chambers and municipal court. The first floor, with large arched bay
doors, was a market featuring "the usual contrivances for hanging up
meat." The market failed and later the fire and police departments
moved in.
Old City Hall Restoration Celebration and 100th anniversary
5/17/91. City Commission and all public City meetings once again
meet on second floor, while first floor rented to Historic Key West
Shipwreck Museum, and then in 1994, to Florida Keys National
Marine Sanctuary.

1892-1899

Jose Marti, Cuba's "George Washington," moves to Key West and begins to raise funds and pick up support for the liberation of Cuba from Spanish reign. He starts the Cuban Revolutionary Party. A passionate orator, Marti delivered his rallying speeches from the balcony of La Terraza de Marti on south Duval.

By 1895, Marti had acquired sufficient economic and volunteer strength to wage the war of liberation and Cuba was attacked. Marti was killed in the first battle.

1898: The *USS Maine*, departs Key West and sails to Havana. The ship is blown up by either a mine or (a new theory) spontaneous combustion resulting from tropically heated wet coal recently loaded in Fort Jefferson. The Spanish-American War begins.

1899: The entire U.S. Atlantic Fleet moves to Key West. The Treaty of Paris ends the war that had spread as far as the Philippines.

1900

Federal Judge J. Vining Harris moves into the almost Southernmost House in the continental United States. At that time, the opulent edifice (constructed for $90,000) was, as Harris had dictated, the "Southernmost."

In 1940, author Thelma Strabel, who wrote *"Reap the Wild Wind"* about the Key West wrecking business, built further south on the southernmost point.

1901

Henry Morrison Flagler's Florida East Coast Railway (FEC) is completed from Jacksonville to Miami. As he built the railroad down the coast, Flagler would erect magnificent hotels in which his passengers would relax and spend money (Ponce de Leon and Alcazar in St. Augustine, Royal Poinciana and the Breakers in Palm Beach and the Royal Palm in Miami). He had absolutely no plans to attempt extension across the sea on down to Key West. That would be ridiculous.

1902

Flagler begins a survey for the FEC in the Everglades.

The Navy, apprehensive about Europe, condemns the southwestern shore of Key West and begins construction of a larger naval base.

Curry and Sons Ice and Electric Plant blows up.

1903

The Coca Cola bottler, one of the first in the country, opens on Simonton Street. The famous secret formula was secretly mixed with collected rainwater as fresh aquifer water from wells was in short supply.

Antonio Diaz Carrasco, Cuban Consul (1903-1915), moves to Key West. Cuba is free.

1904

Henry Flagler (the "Godfather of Florida," Rockefeller's partner, salt magnate from Michigan, Standard Oil baron, rich as all get out) abandons potential FEC Everglades route (too mushy) and hatches this great idea to build the "Overseas Railway" from Miami to Cuba.

THE PLAN: Passengers and freight load up in Miami, enjoy a scenic trip and cross a bunch of bridges on the way down to Key West where the trains run right onto the docks. The regular passengers hop off and jump on awaiting ships while luxurious private passenger cars and freight cars are rolled into the ferries and then sail on down to Havana. THEN... pick up Havana freight, Caribbean produce and passengers from the Panama Canal (still in concept), pack the freight cars, sail back to Key West, hook the cars up as they roll out of the ferry, passengers hop on the train as it pulls out ... and run on up to New York City in 33 hours.

People in Key West love the idea! The rest of the people in the world presume Flagler's elevator doesn't quite make it to the top floor, i.e., "Flagler's Folly."

1905

Milton Curry Mansion (Caroline and Ann Streets) is built on property occupied by his father William's home, which was torn

down. The mansion is Key West's most magnificent home and now is a fascinating museum operated by Al and Edith Amsterdam. Flagler begins construction of the "Overseas Railway."

1906

As construction continues, Flagler is beset by enormous obstacles. The ground is either swamp, hard marl rock or ocean. The laborers hate the work, the mosquitoes love the laborers. There is no fresh water or anything else. No one is exactly sure how to even build the railroad, especially when, later that year, a hurricane destroys everything that they had constructed.

1907

The FEC work force increases to 2,500.

EXPRESS TRAIN CROSSING LONG KEY VIADUCT

Long Key Viaduct is completed; 2¼ miles long, 31 feet above water, 186 concrete arches. The construction is engineered by J.C. Meredith, an expert concerning reinforced concrete structures and the new German cement that hardens underwater.

Zane Grey later traveled to Long Key, via the FEC, to relax on sandy, palm-lined beaches and fish.

1908

The railroad is half-finished. Plans are being invented for the 7 mile ocean span at Marathon, a town so named because it took forever to get there.

FEC WORKCREW LOUNGING AROUND THE HOUSEBOAT

1909

The FEC is on a regular schedule embarking from Knights Key (just south of Marathon) to New York.

Work is progressing on the Seven Mile Bridge. The tracks have to be higher than the highest hurricane waves. Massive pilings are built. Meredith dies and William J. Krome takes over the project.

The work pace is picked up and construction continues into hurricane season. The Seven Mile Bridge is half completed when a hurricane strikes. The bridge, though severely damaged, is structurally OK.

1910

The railroad is well into the Lower Keys when another hurricane hits. Major damage occurs back at the Seven Mile Bridge when the central brace piling is cracked.

The hurricane hits Key West hard with winds over 100 mph. St. Paul's Episcopal Church, Spark's Chapel and the fire house are destroyed.

1911

J.R. Parrot, one of Flagler's foremen, is summoned to build a railroad station and seaport in Key West. There is a small problem however . . . there isn't any land available on the island for Flagler's terminal and shipping yards. With the assistance of Howard Trumbo, Parrot creates the land by a dredge and fill process. Two facing peninsulas, with drawbridge, are produced (Trumbo Point and present day Hilton Haven) to serve as RR roadbed across Garrison Bight. Key West becomes a larger island by approximately 134 acres.

The construction schedule is again pushed up, to 24 hours per day.

J.A.W. McCurdy attempts to fly (can you believe it?) to Havana and is rescued off the Cuban coast.

1912

The railroad reaches Key West at a cost in excess of $50,000,000 and 700 lives.

The terminal includes a 1,700-foot long, 134-foot wide pier with steamships docked alongside.

The first train arrives on January 22 pulling Flagler in his private car "Rambler." A huge celebration, bands, parades, Latin diplomats connected with the Panama Canal (opens 1914) and thousands of Key Westers welcome the Overseas Railway . . . "Eighth Wonder of the World."

1913

Key West population: 23,000.

Flagler dies.

Aviation history is made when the world's first international solo flight is successfully completed between Key West, U.S.A., and Mariel, Cuba. The pilot is Agustin Parla. The native Key Wester is honored with a bust at Key West International Airport.

Hold everything . . . there's another story!

It seems that when Parla first attempted the flight, his seaplane encountered rough seas upon take-off and he abandoned his "history-making" sojourn on the beach near the present day site of the Reach Resort on Key West's southern shore.

While everyone was standing around and moping, a Cuban National named Domingo Rosillo took off from Trumbo Point in Key West and circled over the dejected Parla.

This is when Parla supposedly pulled out a gun and either fired off a couple of rounds at Rosillo or tried to kill himself. In either case, he missed.

Rosillo then flew on down to Havana.

1914-1918

World War I is set in motion as England declares war on Germany.

THE BIG, NOISY GUNS OF FT. TAYLOR

Key West, with its railroad and close proximity to major shipping lanes (25% of worldwide shipping tonnage passes Key West), is activated as strategic center of Caribbean defenses. New piers and radio communications facilities are built. Naval activity in Key West includes destroyers, submarines, aircraft and blimp squadrons as well as supply port and repair facilities.

Thomas Edison experiments with depth charges, stays at the Little White House and never misses a show from his box seat at the Monroe Theater (now The Copa nightclub) movie house.

1919

Meanwhile, construction on the Casa Marina Hotel, begun in 1918, is close to completion.

The architecturally Mediterranean influenced hotel with extravagant grounds is to house happy FEC tourists while they enjoy Key West. Luxurious times were reveled in until the Casa closed after the 1935 hurricane.

WW II: becomes Naval Officer's housing.

THE CASA MARINA AND SURROUNDING NEIGHBORHOOD, LATE 1930's
PLENTY OF PRIME REAL ESTATE STILL AVAILABLE!

1940 / 1950's: Opened and closed.
1962: Army barracks, Cuban Missile Crisis.
Late 1960's: Peace Corps training center.
1978: Restored to full grandeur.

1920

The Kress Building, Key West's first 5¢ & 10¢ store, is built. Fast Buck Freddie's moves in during 1978.

Volstead Act (Prohibition) is enacted. Key West wrecking courts are gasping their final breaths (they close forever in 1921) and the sponging industry is dead. Key West mariners begin looking for new maritime activities.

1921

The Casa Marina opens and fun-loving tourists arrive.

Small, quick vessels, similar to the old wrecking and sponging fleets, depart for Havana and begin smuggling in thousands of cases of bootlegged devil water.

RUMRUNNERS BEING PURSUED BY AND FIRED UPON BY STEAM POWERED COAST GUARD VESSEL

After nearing the shallow mangroves around Key West, the location is noted and the whiskey sunk. The boats then pull into port. Under cover of darkness the contraband would be retrieved and brought ashore. Occasionally, if a daytime delivery was imperative, fires would be started on the north side of Key West and, as the multitudes rushed to the scene, the liquor was off-loaded on the south side.

1922

Automobile, house and jewelry sales are up.

Seven FEC carloads of racehorses arrive from Montreal en route to Havana.

Aeromarine Airways, using converted Navy F-5-L seaplanes, flys passengers and mail to Cuba. The original hanger was located between Simonton and Duval on the Gulf of Mexico where the "flying boats" would take off and land.

1923

The finer points of rumrunning emerge as local captains hide in mangroves, watch where smugglers hide their stash and then steal the liquor before the first smugglers come back for pick up.

AEROMARINE AIRWAYS "FLYING BOAT"

1924-1925

3,500 railroad carloads of pineapples pass through Key West. Ships from Cuba bring in the pineapples and Key West becomes the world's leading supplier of the canned fruit.

Pineapple plantations on Cudjoe and Big Pine Key begin to gear up for the coming pineapple boom. Owners load their first crop onto FEC sidings and a Big Pine town celebration is organized to greet the train. But the FEC doesn't stop and zooms on down to Key West. Cuban pineapples are cheaper.

Later, sweeter and cheaper pineapples from Hawaii finally kill the Florida Keys' business.

PINEAPPLES BEING LOADED ON TRAIN IN KEY WEST

1926

The La Concha Hotel, tallest building in Key West, opens. Mentioned in Hemingway's *"To Have and Have Not"* as the first sight on the approaching horizon of Key West, the hotel also housed such lofty guests as Juan Trippe, president of the soon-to-be Pan Am Airways and Tennessee Williams while he wrote *"Battle of Angels."* The hotel has been restored and re-opened in 1986 by Holiday Inn.

1927

Pan Am launches its first international commercial flight departing from Meacham Field, Key West (site of KW International) bound for Havana. Pan Am's original offices were located in what became the Pigeon House Patio on Whitehead Street. Homing pigeons roosted there until sent along on flights, to be released in the event an emergency message needed to be returned to Key West. In 1993, actress Kelly McGillis opened up "Kelly's" restaurant and southernmost micro brewery at that location.

THE AIR-WAY TO **HAVANA**

PALM BEACH
MIAMI
NASSAU
KEY WEST
HAVANA

PAN AMERICAN AIRWAYS, INC.
PERSHING SQUARE BUILDING
NEW YORK

1928

Several European nations complain that the dredge and fill operations performed by Flagler's FEC Railroad have changed the path of the Gulf Stream, resulting in unusually harsh winters.

1929- 1930

The Depression begins in Key West: business drops, tourists leave, railroad near bankruptcy.

HEMINGWAY HOUSE

1931

Ernest Hemingway moves into a house (Whitehead Street) built by Confederate shipbuilder and Key West Wrecker Asa Tift. Hemingway and second wife Pauline buy the house for $8,000 at a tax sale and later add Key West's first swimming pool.

1932

Hoboes, in record numbers, ride the rails to sunny Key West.

1933-1934

Business is hideous: no sponges, Havana trade off, pineapples gone, Mallory Steamship Line closed, railroad losing money,

FISH PEDDLER, HARD TIMES, 1934

cigar industry gone, Navy decommissioning, over half the locals
on relief and Key West declares bankruptcy.

The City Commission, unable to carry the burden of an
insufficient economic foundation, adopts resolutions placing the
administration of Key West affairs in the hands of Florida
governor Dave Sholtz.

Julius Stone is appointed Florida administrator of the Federal
Emergency Relief Administration. Key West, under FERA
direction, undergoes a unique community planning experiment
and, after 2,000,000 donated manhours of labor, is presented as
THE tourist resort of the American Tropics.

40,000 tourists visit during season in 1935.

1935

Labor Day, Monday, September 2.
Islamorada, 90 miles south of Miami.

Noon: Winds are beginning to gust well over 80 mph,
      the ocean is furious, the sky is bad.
2:22: A foreman for the Florida East Coast Railway is on the
      phone and calls the home office in Miami begging for
      a rescue train to be sent. He has several hundred workers
      and families trapped on the island that's in line for a
      direct hurricane hit.

Although the sun is shining in Miami, the dispatcher is
convinced and, even with the holiday, finally rounds up a crew.

4:25: The rescue train has built steam and departs Miami but
      is held at an open drawbridge allowing vacationing boats
      to pass.

Upon arriving in Homestead the engineer, a veteran of big storms in the Keys, decides to relocate his locomotive to the rear of the train and back down to Islamorada. When the storm victims are finally loaded, he will then be able to pull the train at a greater speed back up the Keys to the mainland.

5:15: Rescue train departs Homestead and backs towards Islamorada, 60 miles away.

6:50: The train stops at Snake Creek, now well under the hurricane's seige, to pick up refugees. A broken cable lashing about in the wind fouls the engine cab. It takes over an hour to cut it free.

8:10: Very dark; winds gusting to 200 mph; 10 foot waves breaking over the tracks.

This is a Force 5 hurricane that generates forces on par with an atomic bomb. The barometer drops to 26:35 inches, the lowest reading ever in the Western hemisphere.

8:20: The engineer, unable to see through the walls of raining water, overshoots Islamorada and has to pull back to the station.

Twenty miles down the tracks at Marathon, waves in the open channels are peaking at 20 feet as wind gusts pass 250 mph.

With only the headlight of the locomotive to illuminate the surreal scene, terrified survivors begin to scramble onto the rescue train.

Five minutes later a 17-foot tidal wave buries everything and washes the island bare. The death toll is unknown, however, 600 bodies were recovered.

The "Overseas Railroad" disappears.

1936-1938

Key West, having suffered little damage from the hurricane, is now without ground transportation to the mainland for the first time since 1912.

While the storm had washed away tracks, it did not damage the bridges. The FEC sold the track beds to the government and the Overseas Highway started under the direction of B. M. Duncan.

The highway paved over roadbeds and long beams were stradled across pilings to allow for the wider automobile bridges.

The Overseas Highway was completed in 1938 and re-financed with a one dollar toll.

1939

Franklin D. Roosevelt rides the highway and visits Key West.

The last large sailing vessel built in Key West, the *Western Union,* is built and launched by Western Union Telegraph Co. The ship is used to check and repair Key West/Cuba submerged signal cable.

1940

Karl von Cosel, an X-ray technician, is arrested after the discovery of his true love Elena Hoyas Mesa's body in his house. She had died 7 years earlier, had been exhumed, preserved, elegantly dressed and laid in bed.

Welcome to the "Twilight Zone."

1941-1945

World War II is underway and German submarine activity threatens Caribbean shipping lanes. Over 100 Allied ships are torpedoed in the Straits of Florida.

15,000 service personnel and their families are stationed in Key West.

The Gulf Control Center is activated with aircraft, Navy and Coast Guard ships, blimps and the civilian Coast Guard to patrol the Straits and the Gulf. Minefields are laid to protect harbored convoys of merchant marines.

Roving German U-boats disappear and the torpedo attacks cease.

NAVY DAY PARADE, 1943
DUVAL STREET, KEY WEST

1946-1948

President Harry Truman visits the Little White House. Truman enjoyed 11 "working vacations" in Key West and was the most frequent Presidential visitor. He endeared himself to locals with his informal attitudes (he ate breakfast at Shorty's Diner), poker sessions, piano playing and penchant for Hawaiian shirts.

1949

While evidence seemed to suggest that there must be shrimp out there, Key West catches always came up puny. Everywhere else on the coast shrimpers went out and, after a day of trawling nets . . . shrimp!

Then one night, as Norberg Thompson's boat lay broken and adrift off the Dry Tortugas, the crew put the nets out to pass the time. The next morning . . . "PINK GOLD." Big, fat jumbo shrimp! It turned out that the shrimp hated the light penetrating the Keys' clear waters and came up only after dark.

Realizing this could be bigger than the sponging business, locals decided to keep it secret. However, after masses of shrimp began

to suddenly appear at coastal fish markets, the word got out (O.K., who told?) and hundreds of shrimp boats from North Carolina to Texas swarmed to Key West.

Typically, a 3-man crew will spend up to two weeks hunting at sea for shrimp. Sometimes they pull up things "bigger than Peterbilt trucks." The catch is cooled with ice as conventional freezing destroys the membranes. There is, however, a process practiced on "freezer boats" where the shrimp, contained in netted bags, are dipped in a brine solution and quick frozen. They taste great!

1950-1954

The "Marine Gold Rush" is on!
The shrimp grounds now total more than one hundred square

miles and drift between Key West and the Dry Tortugas. By February, 1950, one week's catch weighs in at 253,000 pounds, including one triumphant trawler's haul of 44,000 pounds. The jumbo shrimp wholesale at 55 cents per pound.

Norberg Thompson, the man who started it all and one of Key West's most industrious citizens (he owned and ran the sponging business and positioned Key West sponges in the world market, a turtle fishing fleet and canning company that shipped worldwide, the Key West Cigar Box Factory, Thompson's Fish Company, Thompson's Ice Company, a shipping company that built the largest four-masted sailing schooner in the world, a trucking company that hauled every piece of freight between Key West and Miami, the largest hardware store south of Miami, a pineapple plantation and guava jelly factory. During his spare time, Mr. Thompson served on both the City and County Commissions, the Overseas Highway Committee, the Everglades National Park Commission and, even when he protested, was drafted and elected Mayor by an overwhelming majority of Key Westers... whew!). Anyway, Thompson's Seafood starts up, hires 100 women to behead the shrimp and begins processing the local catch.

By 1954, the shrimp industry, with as many as 500 vessels, is pulling in over 30 million pounds of "Key West Pinks" per year.

1955

Tennessee Williams wins the Pulitzer Prize for "Rose Tattoo."
"Tennessee" (Thomas Lanier) first visited Key West in 1941 and resided at the Tradewinds Boarding House. In 1949, he bought a small, white clapboard house and moved it from Bahama Street to Duncan Street, at the edge of some mangrove swamps. Later he added a pool (he found swimming to be very therapeutic), a writing studio, a guest house, a gazebo given to him by Gloria Swanson (for bridge), a picket fence and painted the shutters red.

Many, many authors have been smitten with Key West's wily ways, resulting in more pounds per square inch of literary Pulitzer Prize winners living here than anywhere else in the world.

Authors who have lived in Key West and the Keys include:
Robert Porter Allen, Ellis Amburn, John J. Audubon, Fred Belland, Elizabeth Bishop, Marie-Claire Blais, James Boatwright, Alma Bond, Rosalind Brackenburg, John Malcolm Brinnin, Jimmy Buffett, Ned Buntline, Philip Burton, Truman Capote, Phil Caputo, Jean Carper, Virginia Spencer Carr, John Ciardi, Thomas Cockrell, John N. Cole, Kirby Congdon, Parley Cooper, Bill Cosford, Marie Cosindas, Bonnie Costello, Elmer Davis, Love Dean, Tana de Gamez, Barbara Deming, Annie Dillard, Scott Donaldson, John Dos Passos, Dick Duane, Barbara Ehrenreich, Kathleen Elgin, Desmond Eliot, Ralph Ellison, Michael Evans, Jeffrey A. Fisher, Robert C. Fisher, Nancy Friday, Robert Frost, Burt Garnett, Jay Garon, Robert Allen Green, Zane Grey, James Hall, Ruth Harris, Jim Harrison, Ralph Hayes, David Heller, Deane Fons Heller, Ernest Hemingway, James Leo Herlihy, Jerry Herman, John Hersey, Carl Hiaasen, L. Rust Hills, Burt Hirschfeld, Edward Hower, Colin Jameson, David Kaufelt, Lynn Kaufelt, Judith Kazentis, Stetson Kennedy, Kathleen Kilgore, James Kirkwood, Lorenzo de Kleinhans, Albin Krebs, Harriet La Barre, Joan Langley, Wright Langley, Joseph P. Lash, John Leslie, Harriet Liens, Frances & Richard Lockridge, David Loovis, Alison Lurie, John D. McDonald, Thomas McGuane, Rollie McKenna, W.H. Manville, James Merrill, Arthur S. Miller, John (aka John Royce) Mitchell, Lilian Mowrer, Ralph Middleton Munroe, Kirk Munroe, George Murphy, Susan Nadler, Clarke Newlon, Stephen Nichols, Charlotte Niedhauk, Jane O'Reilly, Don Pinder, Darwin Porter, T.D. Press, Kathryn Hall Proby, Evan Rhodes, Robert Richardson, William Roos, Norman Rosten, Anne E. Rowe, Leigh W. Rutledge, Thomas Sanchez, Budd Schulberg, Richard Alan Schwartz, Mary Lee Settle, Laurence Shames, Shel Silverstein, Micky Spillane, Stanwood Russell Sterling, Ramona Stewart, Wallace Stevens, Robert Stone, Thelma Strabel, Mr. & Mrs. Arnold Sundgaard, Gloria Swanson, Frank Taylor, Peter Taylor, Robert L. Taylor, Harry S Truman, John Viele, Irving Weinman, Hyman Weitzen, Sharon Wells, Janwillem van de Weterling, Steve Whalen, Louise White, Richard Wilbur, John Edward Williams, Joy Williams, William Wright, Tennessee Williams and Benedict Thielen, who pegged the island best when he noted, "Key West is a place where the unexpected happens with monotonous regularity."

PHOTO BY ED SWIFT, JR.

AERIAL VIEW OF KEY WEST, 1956

1956

Angry Key Westers complain about the stink arising from the dried up, decaying salt ponds, which are now evolving into a 300-acre mosquito breeding ground. Culverts allowing tidal waterflow, closed during development, are re-opened.

Teenagers are restricted by a 9 PM curfew, signaled by the ringing of the Waddell Bell atop Old City Hall.

Secretary of State John Foster Dulles recuperates in Key West ("My, this sunshine sure feels good!") and is visited by Vice-President Richard Nixon.

A hound dog named "Paddlefoot" sniffs out convicted murderer Willie Wilson and "Cissie," from Cudjoe Key, makes dog medical history by surviving two rattlesnake bites.

The *SS City of Havana* ferry launches service, 3 days per week, to Havana and Key West becomes one of the country's leading ports of foreign travel, averaging 12,900 passengers a month.

1957

A mysterious "yellow blight" disease decimates Key West coconut palms. The plague was first noticed in late 1955 when the palm fronds began to turn yellow, fall off and then the trees died. No one could figure it out, much less stop the devastation. Within 18 months 8,000 coconut palm trees die in Key West. Tropically foliaged landscapes are exterminated. By the time scientists determine that the disease had begun in Jamaica and is caused by lethal microbes (micoplasma-like organisms, or MLO's) spread by insects called planthoppers, the blight has moved up the mainland and by 1974 has destroyed 90% of the coconut palms in Miami. By 1978 the disease, now called "lethal yellowing," has crossed the Gulf of Mexico where it destroys the lower Rio Grande Valley's date palms. Currently the blight is marching through the Yucatan Peninsula and threatens Mexico's coconut industry. Although there is a treatment to suppress the symptoms, there is no cure. Once treatment stops . . . the palms die. Fortunately the Malayan Dwarf palms, reaching heights of 60 feet and maturing in 3 to 4 years, have proven to be resistant to "LY." New plantings are again putting the swaying palms back into tropical environments.

Meanwhile, the City of Key West bans outhouses.

1958

The Conch Tour Train begins the first sightseeing tours of Key West. Longer than a semi, the trains somehow successfully navigate the city's narrow streets.

Former President Herbert Hoover arrives for his annual mid-winter bonefishing outing.

The Casa Marina hosts a baseball convention attended by, among others, Mickey Mantle, Stan Musial, Robin Roberts and Bob Turley. Mrs. Harry Lee Baker is hit by a foul ball during batting practice before the all-star game.

A revolution, of sorts, begins on Cuba's eastern coast. Hemingway, while in Havana, reports heightened military police surveillance. Mayor Delio Cobo, accompanied by city officials, visits Cuban President Fulgenico Batista in Havana and is assured that Fidel Castro's aggravating revolution poses no real threat. Key West police break up an anti-Batista parade involving over 40 autos. Ten Castro supporters, smuggling over $50,000 in arms, are intercepted and arrested in Key West. As the revolution matures, American tourists departing from Key West are arrested in Havana. No reasons are given.

1959

On January 1, Batista abruptly surrenders to Castro rebels. The dictatorship is defunct.

Refugees immediately begin to emigrate to Key West and 500 Castro supporters take the return trip back to Cuba on the *SS City of Havana* ferry. Cuban Senator Rolando Masferer arrives in Key West Harbor with a reportedly smuggled 17 million dollars.

Aerovias Q Airlines resumes regular scheduled flights to Havana as Castro welcomes American tourists. Cuban reform policies of democracy, honest government and social justices are initiated. Castro reiterates his stand against communism and its socialist system.

Cary Grant and Tony Curtis arrive for the filming of "Operation Petticoat." The superstructure of the U.S. submarine *Balao* is repainted pink.

Commandante Camilo Cienfueges arrives in Key West with Castro look-a-likes for a meeting at San Carlos. Castro's "good neighbor" policy is endorsed by Havana businessmen and the Key West Chamber of Commerce.

1960

Castro establishes diplomatic relations with the USSR and then declares that the Cuban Revolution had been, indeed, a socialist rebellion.

What happened?

Castro, ripe with revolutionary success, began to view himself as a champion for Third World nations. The U.S. had long supported dictatorships in Latin America (in 1958 Vice-President Nixon, on a goodwill tour of eight Latin American nations, had been greeted with hostility by angry mobs in all countries except Samoza's Nicaragua). When Castro began to nationalize Cuban industry and agrarian enterprises without compensation, the U.S. protested the economic and social "reforms."

Fearing U.S. retaliation, Castro turned to Russia for protection. That worked for a while, until the Russkies put the screws on and mandated that Cuba adopt communist policies in return for defensive capabilities.

Castro gets his custodial muscle and the USSR brings the Cold War to the Western Hemisphere.

1961

Castro is firmly in control of Communist Cuba and the United States slams the diplomatic door. U.S. trade with Cuba is now forbidden and the economic effects begin to sabotage the local Key West economy. The La Concha Hotel closes and the civilian airport deteriorates. American-born Cubans ban Cuban programs at San Carlos; the City Commission outlaws the Cuban flag from Old City Hall. The Associated Press opens a local office in Key West. The U.S. supported Bay of Pigs invasion of Cuba is resoundingly repelled.

1962

October 15: A U.S. U-2 high altitude surveillance aircraft produces clear photos pinpointing Soviet ballistic missile locations in Cuba.

October 19: Marines begin LST maneuvers in Key West Harbor. Twelve Phantom jets arrive at the Naval Air Station "on their way to participate in naval exercises in Puerto Rico.'

October 20: Rumors begin to spread that the Overseas Highway will close and a civilian evacuation is imminent. Russian submarines are observed surfacing in the Straits of Florida.

October 21: U.S. Ambassador Adlai Stevenson addresses the UN Security Council and warns that Soviet weapons must go. Soviets counter that NATO based missiles must be removed from Italy and Turkey.

October 22: President John F. Kennedy addresses the nation on television. Unless the Russians immediately begin to cease all deliveries and remove their nuclear warheads, the United States will quarantine Cuba. All Soviet ships transporting offensive weapons will be intercepted and ordered to turn back

October 23: At a national press conference:
Question: "How many ships, aircraft and personnel does the U.S. have in the Key West area?"
Answer: "We have more than enough."

October 24: At 10 AM the United States Second Fleet, now
based out of Key West, and under the command of
Admiral George W. Anderson, moves into position
with 183 naval vessels to quarantine Cuba. Surveillance
indicates that Soviet ships carrying offensive weapons are
3 days out.

Secretary of Defense Robert McNamara is authorized
to call up 150,000 reserves.

October 26: The "Today Show" brings a crew to Key West
and while on a tour of Duval Street, broadcasts "lack
of panic, business as usual." Locals theorize that if missiles
are launched from Cuba, the arc of their flight path
is such that they will pass over Key West.

U.S. Army convoy arrives.

October 27: The worst day. A Soviet surface-to-air (SAM)
missile shoots down a U-2 spy plane over Cuba. There
are two stories on how this happened. One: Communist
Cubans, fed up with Soviet procrastination, attacked and
conquered the Russian SAM base and hysterically fired
the missile. Two: Soviet troops fired without authority.
Tensions accelerated; the planet is on the verge of nuclear
holocaust as verification of Soviet intentions is unclear.
Kennedy decides to exercise patience.

October 28: "We're eyeball to eyeball, and I think the other
fellow just blinked," said Dean Rusk, Secretary of State.

Khrushchev yields to Kennedy's demands; incoming
Soviet ships with offensive weapons turn back and
missiles are withdrawn.

November 20: Blockade of Cuba cancelled, tourist business in
Key West rebounds.

November 26: President Kennedy visits Key West in a
whirlwind tour that lasts less than 2 hours. He is
accompanied by Florida Governor Farris Bryant,
Congressman Dante Fascell and every big-brass admiral
and general from the Pentagon. Several problems arise
when Key West dogs become too jubilant and the
zooming motorcade has to swerve around them. To
complicate matters further, celebrating citizens are
pitched into an even higher partying frenzy when word
hits the streets that an All Girl Band will arrive for the
big street dance later in the week. Mayor C.B. Harvey has
barely enough time to present the President with the Key
to the City before he heads back to Washington D.C.

Later in the week: Former Vice President Richard Nixon arrives.

1963

The new City Hall opens on Angela Street. Controversy arises as costs have escalated from the contracted $315,000 to $336,000. Key West Handprint Fabrics donates 500 yards of drapery material. City Manager Archie Lowe goes on a spending orgy to furnish new offices and is fired by the City Commission.

The Gulf Oil waterfront property between Duval and Simonton Streets is sold to developer David W. Wolkowsky for $106,000. Wolkowsky presents plans for a boat basin, hotel and cabana club to be called the Pier House.

1964

The Beatles fly into Key West, loll around in cabanas and swim at the Key Wester Motel. After their departure, "Beatled" pool water is sold for big bucks at the Navy Charity Auction.

Four Cuban fishing boats are seized in U.S. territorial waters. A trial is held in Key West under the jurisdiction of Florida and Cuban captains are fined $500. Castro retaliates by cutting off water to the Guantanamo Naval Base. The Navy cuts the pipes and re-routes the water supply.

"Escape from Hell Island" is filmed in Key West.

1965

Castro initiates an open door policy and 6,000 Cuban refugees pour into family arms in Key West.

Hurricane Betsy slams Key West with $300,000 in damages.

The Causeway across Garrison Bight opens creating a long overdue circular traffic route through the island. Construction begins on "Searstown."

Florida State Representative Bernie Papy, Jr. introduces legislation calling for a $100 fine to be levied against anyone advertising Key Lime Pie that is not made with key limes. Key Lime Pie has long been a stape of island cuisine since its creation eons ago ... or maybe it was in the '40's.

Meanwhile, Key West has its first BIG bank robbery. To begin with, the robbers set a fire in town so that the arriving fire engines and crowds would create enough racket to cover up the noise of the break into Florida Keys First National Bank and subsequent concrete hammer drilling through the second floor. After 15 hours of acetylene torching, the top of the safe was lifted off. Fortunately for the robbers, this was a weekend job. Once inside the safe, the thieves apparently took a sandwich break (one works up a powerful appetite in the bank robbery business) before rifling through the safe deposit boxes and stealing an undeterminable fortune. The crime remains unsolved.

1966

Hurricanes Alma and Inez, Garry Moore, Jimmy Hoffa, Vice-President Hubert "Happy" Humphrey, Jayne Mansfield (appearing at the Tradewinds supper club) and a Honduran cucumber ship visit Key West.

Three flying saucers are seen over Mallory Docks and a black ooze discovered on 13th Street is declared explosive.

1967

Fresh clean water has always been of critical importance to Key Westers. The island sits on a limestone base and digging wells down to the aquifer proved to be a major undertaking.

In the old days the collection of rain served as the primary source for drinkable water. One reason the roofs in Old Town sport so many peaks is so that more surface is exposed to collect the rain. After the fire of 1886, tin roofs were initially installed to protect against flying sparks. However, the new roofs proved even more beneficial by channeling, via downspouts, cleaner water into cisterns. Water would then be hauled around town by mule-drawn carts.

WATER DELIVERY, CUSTOM SERVICE

Key West averages 40 inches of rain per year; it's the driest city in south Florida. Additional fresh water was always in demand.

In 1942 the Florida Keys Aqueduct Authority and the Navy joined in partnership to build a 138-mile long pipeline from Florida City to Key West.

By 1967 Westinghouse had completed the country's largest desalinization plant, which produced 2.6 million gallons of fresh water daily from sea water. The plant operated on expensive diesel fuel and was mothballed in 1983.

Meanwhile, FKAA began to enlarge the water pipeline from 18 inches in diameter to, in some areas, 30 inches.

1968

An ominous trend sets its course when the Navy decommissions the ship repair facilities and apprenticeship program and then fires 240 civilian employees. The Navy has been the backbone of Key West's economic health and locals begin to worry.

1969

Sportfishing charter boats move to new docking facilities below the Garrison Bight Causeway. Up until this point the boats docked along U.S. 1 at Garrison Bight creating traffic problems when displaying their impressive daily catch. The waters of Key West contain over 600 varieties of fish and offer, according to <u>Sports Illustrated</u>, "an incomparable fishing ground."

Sportfishing generally means you let the fish go. Most mounted fish today are made of plastic.

One little thing to clear up about "dolphin." The ones we eat, sometimes referred to as "Mahi Mahi" are the fish, not the mammals.

PHOTO BY ED SWIFT, JR.

FISHING GUIDE ROY LOWE DEMONSTRATES REAL SPORTFISHIN! YOU TAKE A HUNK OF MEAT, BIG HOOK, 3 FEET OF CHAIN, 6 FEET OF DOUBLE COILED ROPE... THROW IT IN THE WATER AND... WHAM! THEN SIMPLY PULL IN A 400 POUND TIGER SHARK. (PHOTO 1953)

1970

Rear Admiral F.J. Brush explains to local business leaders that, due to the 1971 U.S. Fiscal Budget, cutbacks are coming and the military / civilian complex may suffer up to a $6,000,000 payroll loss. The city begins to fear the worst.

1971

Key West is the number one seaport destination for imported cucumbers. A large shipment of bees arrive at Mallory Square, some escape and a beekeeper is hired to round up the strays.

A ban is placed on catching sea turtles measuring less than 41 inches in length. This effectively puts an end to the business.

CAPTAIN ALLIE EBANKS (IN STRAW HAT), OF THE TURTLE SCHOONER *A.M. ADAMS* FROM GRAND CAYMEN, GETS HELP FROM EVERYBODY AS THEY LOWER A VERY LARGE GREEN INTO A DISPLAY TANK.

For hundreds of years, the easygoing sea creatures had been a food staple of Caribbean natives.

Green turtles, some up to four feet across and weighing up to 500 pounds, were netted in waters as far away as Nicaragua. After being hoisted up on to the schooner's deck, the greens were stored laying on their backs with flippers tied and periodically splashed with sea water. Hawksbill turtles would be harpooned when they surfaced to breathe. The harpoon would pierce just below the shell so as not to kill the animal.

Upon arrival in Key West the turtles would be held in tidal flushed corrals at the Turtle Kraals and butchered as needed.

Turtle meat was then cut into steaks (tastes something like . . . chicken!), ground into turtle burgers or used in chowder. The soft belly, shell and flippers were processed into soup, first canned in 1895.

Sea turtles have now been declared an endangered species and are passionately protected by the U.S. government.

1972

Key West begins a major transitional period that premiers with paradoxical circumstances including continued major military cutbacks of marine activities, an antiquated sewer system declared obsolete by the state, racial unrest started by two high school kids, feuds between local businessmen, Hurricane Agnes,

SQUARE GROUPER HARVEST

Dustin Hoffman, and, spurred by local drug smugglers, the best business year ever.

The Florida Legislature creates the Historic Key West Preservation Board to research, acquire, restore and maintain all aspects of Key West's historic sites, buildings and properties. Retired Navy Captain John Higgins is appointed director. In 1977 former "Miami Herald" Keys Bureau Chief and author Wright Langley is appointed director and in 1985 the agency changes its name to the Historic Florida Keys Preservation Board.

1973

All submarine activity in Key West is discontinued, 14 acres of the Naval Station are declared surplus, gasoline rationing pulverizes the tourist economy, Duval Street merchants and bars are crippled, police and hippies skirmish at Mallory Square, record shrimp catches are reported and Burl Ives arrives to do a television documentary about Tennessee Williams.

1974

Nixon decommissions the Naval Station, the last inspection is held, the flag is lowered, the base is closed. Demolition begins on military housing at Peary Court and 97 acres on the base are declared surplus.

Key West's main street, Duval, goes bankrupt and 90% of all businesses, mostly bars, close their doors. This place is a ghost town.

City government and business leaders initiate plans to revitalize the local economy by shifting the emphasis from the military to the tourist business. "Key West, The American Tropics, Tourist Destination," first successfully implemented by the FERA in 1934, is back on the drawing boards. The goal is to be in operation by the "1976 Bicentennial."

1975

The Naval Base is renamed the Harry S. Truman Annex and offered for sale by the federal government.

Advance federal aid of $603,000 for the "Downtown '76" project arrives and another $1,100,000 is on the way.

615 DUVAL STREET, BEFORE RESTORATION

Old Town Key West Development, a private firm, begins the rehabilitation of buildings on Duval Street with designs sensitive to Key West's architectural heritage. City-sponsored antique street lamps and bricked crosswalks combine with tree plantings to snazz up the blighted area. The process will continue until 1980. In 1983 OTKWD will receive the prestigious Phoenix Award for historical neighborhood restoration. This will be the first time an American private firm has won the international award.

615 DUVAL STREET, AFTER RESTORATION

1976

The city is in the midst of massive rehabilitation, Mayor McCoy heads to Washington to discuss a city lease of Truman Annex, Old City Hall receives a new bell tower and roof, the shrimping business is great.

Fire Chief Bum Farto disappears after a drug conviction.

1977

City and Navy reach agreement on a lease of Truman Annex.

The Federal Government allocates $1,200,000 for Key West International Airport improvements.

The Spottswood family sells the Casa Marina to investors and the Casa is restored to full grandeur in 1978.

"Operation Haircut" stifles the drug trade.

Mr. and Mrs. Stanley E. Russell donate their Elvis archives to the Monroe County Public Library.

1978

Mayor Charles "Sonny" McCoy, after conferring with the State Department and receiving President Carter's best wishes, plans an international goodwill campaign to Cuba. Departing Key West Harbor on September 10th on one ski, towed by Captain Sherman Bywater's 58-foot Hatteras *Bullwinkle,* McCoy waterskis to Havana Harbor in 6 hours and 10 minutes, where he is met and escorted by two Cuban gunboats. From there they travel to Mariel and are joined by 50 U.S. mayors who fly in from Atlanta. The municipal dignitaries hang out on the docks, drink daiquiris and eat caviar.

MAYOR SONNY McCOY, ALWAYS THE SNAPPY DRESSER, BEING ESCORTED BY CUBAN GUNBOAT INTO HAVANA HARBOR.

Monroe County Sheriff William Freeman purchases ten new patrol cars using confiscated drug smuggling vehicles and boats for the trade-ins.

Key West prisoners go on a hunger strike the morning of December 10, but call it off just before lunch.

1979

Ms. Jessie Porter Newton, a founder of the Old Island Restoration Foundation, passes away.

The OIRF, founded in 1960, sprang into existence with the catalytic help of the Mitchell Wolfson family who restored the Audubon House.

THE CONVENT OF MARY IMMACULATE, BUILT IN 1875, WAS TORN DOWN IN 1968 BEFORE THE O.I.R.F. WAS SECURELY ESTABLISHED. BUILT FROM NATIVE CORAL ROCK, THE BUILDING WAS SUFFERING FROM ROTTING PORCHES AND DILAPIDATED WIRING. THOUGH RENOVATION COSTS WERE ESTIMATED AT ONLY $100,000; A MORE MODERN CONVENT AND SCHOOL WERE BUILT FOR $600,000.

Dedicated to preserving Key West's landmarks, architecture and lore, the group is affiliated with the National Trust for Historic Preservation which was chartered by Congress to safeguard America's historic heritage.

Every year, the OIRF sponsors Old Island Days, a four-month festival highlighted by the "Red Shawler" ladies, so named for the red wool shawls waved in days gone by to welcome home returning sea captains.

With a membership of over 700, the non-profit organization heroically has raised hundreds of thousands of dollars and spent them on helping to restore Mallory Square, both Martello forts, the Wrecker's Museum, the Key West Woman's Club and Old City Hall.

1980

The Mariel boatlift has its beginnings in early spring when the first Cuban refugees reach Key West. By April 24, the city is on alert that a mass exodus is impending. The U.S. warns against any sort of cooperation, but by April 27, arrivals pass 2,500. Spring storms create a deadly havoc for the vessels and the Coast Guard begins relaying horror stories from the Straits of Florida.

May 2: 1,700 fugitives land in Key West.

May 3: Mobs storm the U.S. Mission in Cuba and returning rescue boats appear on the horizon lining up to enter Key West Harbor.

May 6: President Carter, citing his basic human rights policy, opens the doors for immigration. Families will be reunited, some after 21 years of separation. 6,000 Cuban escapees arrive while an estimated 100,000 wait in Mariel.

May 13: By now the sealift is out of control as hundreds of lobster, shrimping, sportfishing and any other navigable boat become involved. Anxious families are paying up to $1,000 for passage of relatives. Returning captains complain about forced extended layovers, huge extortionary payments to Mariel officials and required extraditions of criminals from Cuban jails.

Docks at Truman Annex are besieged with immigrants and the old seaplane ramps on Trumbo Point are turned into tent cities.

May 15: Carter orders the flotilla to halt, but by May 21 the
total passes 61,000. Boat captains who persist
in participating, some only for profit, are warned their
vessels will be seized and that they will be indicted.

All commercial fishing and shrimping is prohibited
in the Straits of Florida.

June 4: The 100,000th refugee reaches Key West and the influx
continues until July 1.

The Mariel refugees are loaded onto buses and taken
to Miami for immigration processing and the criminals
are incarcerated.

1981

The Key West Aquarium, the town's first tourist attraction,
is restored and re-opens.

It was originally built with federal funds by the FERA in 1934
to assist in revitalizing the tourist industry. It premiered as the
world's first open air aquarium and featured salt water display
tanks which were illuminated and heated by sunlight. Rainbow
colored tropical fish, octopuses, sea turtles, sting rays and sharks
flabbergasted the tourists.

The exhibits have been expanded and research programs
continue.

1982

The United States Border Patrol sets up a military roadblock on U.S. 1, the only road out of the Keys, at Florida City. All northbound traffic is stopped and searched for aliens, guns and drugs. A 19-mile long traffic jam soon evolves and is publicized throughout the venues of all of the major news media.

Key West's tourist business becomes extinct.

As locals gather in deserted public saloons and moan on about the seige, a small group of local businessmen and officials whom shall remain nameless (Dennis Bitner, William E. Smith, Edwin O. Swift III, Townsend Keiffer, John Magliola and Mayor Dennis Wardlow) assemble in the smoke filled back room of FM107. A plan . . . a desperate plan . . . is hatched. Revolution!

The six "Conch Reveres" take to the streets and the nearby wailing cantinas to muster support. After a "couple" of drinks, the newly recruited and now rabid mob votes to secede from the Union and declare war on the United States of America.

The "Conch Republic" is born and, after a few boisterous speeches and ambassadorship appointments, immediately surrenders to the U.S. and applies for foreign aid.

The roadblock is lifted.

SCRIPT: "BENEATH THE 12 MILE REEF" . . . page 22
(AT GREEK SPONGER'S BAR, TARPON SPRINGS)

GREEK (J. Carroll Nash): WAIT, WAIT . . . YOU GONNA SEE . . . NEXT TIME WE GO OUT, WE GONNA COME HOME WITH A FULL LOAD.

MIKE (GILBERT ROLAND): YEA . . . HE'S RIGHT . . . WHERE WE'RE GOING . . . WE'LL GET A FULL LOAD!

GREEK: HEY MIKE, WAIT MIKE . . . FULL LOAD OF SPONGES? WHAT YOU MEAN? YOU MEAN WE GO TO 12 MILE REEF, IS THAT WHAT YOU SAY?

MIKE: WHO SAID 12 MILE REEF? WE'RE GOING TO PICK THE KEYS!!!

GREEK: MIKE, WHAT'S THE MATTER WITH YOU MIKE . . . YOU FORGET THE HOOK BOATS.

TONY (ROBERT WAGNER): WHO'S SCARED OF HOOK BOATS!?!

GREEK: ME . . . SOCRATES OHOOLARIS! I'M SCARED! WE DON'T BELONG IN THE KEYS!!

TONY: WHO SAID SO!?!

GREEK: TONY, YOU DON'T UNDERSTAND . . . LONG TIME AGO, BEFORE YOU BORN . . . YOUR PAPA, ME, PLENTY OTHER GREEKS . . . WE COME TO TARPON AND THE ENGLISHMEN GO TO KEY WEST . . . AND THEY WORK THE KEYS!

TONY: THE CONCHEADS!!!!

GREEK: IN THE OLD DAYS THERE'S A PLENTY SPONGES . . . ANY PLACE YOU GO ENOUGH FOR EVERYBODY, WE DON'T HAVE NO TROUBLE, BUT NOW ALL THE BAGS ARE PICKED . . . IS NO SPONGE LEFT EXCEPT IN DEEP WATER, LIKE 12 MILE REEF . . . OR GLADES . . . BUT THE CONCHS, ENGLISH . . .**1**

1 FROM: "BENEATH THE 12 MILE REEF", DIRECTED BY: ROBERT D. WEBB ©1953, 20th CENTURY FOX

1983

By the 1930's the sponging industry began to creep back and today represents a $1,500,000 business. Unmolested monstrous

sponges in the ship channels had set their spores adrift on the currents, resulting in the re-emergence of sponge beds.

Once again, Conchs and Greeks clash over sponging rights and harvesting techniques. Back in 1953, *"Beneath the 12-Mile Reef,"* filmed in Key West, presented the Hollywood version and by 1983, the 'discussion' had reached the Florida Legislature. The Conchs won.

The Florida Keys remain as the only area in the country where diving for sponges is illegal. They are still hooked, or missed, in average depths of from 4 to 20 feet. The width between the three-pronged hooks has been widened so that immature sponges cannot be taken.

Major varieties harvested today include the sheepswool and glove. They compare very favorably to their Mediterranean counterparts. Once ashore, the yellow sponges are cleaned, dried, clipped and graded, then threaded on strings for sale. Leading uses include cleaning, bathing and slurping up spilled water.

1984

Captain J.B. "Red" Best, commanding officer of the Naval Air Station, announces the Navy will begin to return in force to Key West. The island will become the strategic center of the U.S. Caribbean Task Force.

Construction begins on a new Mallory Dock, to serve as a cultural center for Key West's world famous "sunset celebration" and to provide secure dockage for visiting cruise ships.

1985

One of the greatest adventure stories of the 20th century climaxes after a 16-year search when Mel Fisher and the Treasure Salvors find the multimillion dollar treasure of the *Nuestra Señora de Atocha.*

Legend and lore had it that the *Atocha*, a Havana built Spanish galleon, departed Havana in 1622 loaded to the hilt with gold, silver and gems. The cargo was rumored to be the bulk of Spanish wealth reaped from years of exploitation of Central and South American countries.

A massive hurricane sank the ship somewhere near Key West after two days at sea.

In 1969, Fisher decided to begin the search.

1970: Fisher colleague, Dr. Eugene Lyon, while studying at the Archives of Seville in Spain, happened across the original manifest of the Atocha. The ship is reported to have sunk in the vicinity of the Marquesas Keys, 22 miles from Key West, and is indeed a floating/sinking Fort Knox.

The hunt takes its direction.

1971: A huge anchor, similar to the type that would be carried by the Spanish galleon, is located.

1973: In an area known as the quicksands more than 1,500 silver pieces of eight are found, then a navigational astrolabe and then, gold medallions. When three 70-pound silver bars are salvaged and the serial numbers and weights match numbers on the original manifest, the *Atocha* treasure seems at hand.

Nothing much is turned up for the next two years, except government agents.

1975: State and federal governments lay claim to Mel's treasure, citing public domain.

Bronze cannons are found and documented to be from the *Atocha* manifest.

Tragedy strikes. Mel's son Dirk, Dirk's wife Angel and diver Rick Gage perish when their boat, on location, springs a leak during the night and capsizes.

During the following years the area is searched, but yields little.

1980: Fisher goes back to an area that has indicated strong possibilities and locates an *Atocha* sister ship, the *Margarita.* Long chains of golden links, artifacts and relics of the 17th century are retrieved.

The archeological information is documented.

More and more gold is uncovered.

By 1982, the hunt has brought in $20,000,000 in treasure.

1982: The U.S. Supreme Court rules (5-4) that not only does the treasure belong to Fisher, but that the wreck is to be placed under the jurisdition of the U.S. District Court.

Mel decides to divide his salvage forces and resume the search for the *Atocha*. Archeologist Duncan Mathewson has developed a theory that when the *Atocha* sank, the wreck was swept along the sea bottom by strong storm currents. The trail turns up fragments of treasure but eventually peters out. The divers backtrack.

1985: During May, 13 solid gold bars and 16 extraordinary emeralds in gold settings are brought up.

On July 20 divers discover the "MOTHERLODE" directly beneath their boat. Silver bars are piled like a reef, protected by lobsters.

By August tons of silver bars, thousands of coins, 200 pounds of gold bars, chains, medallions and $60,000,000 in exquisite Columbian emeralds are hauled into Treasure Salvor headquarters.

A HAPPY MEL FISHER ATTIRED IN "SEVERAL" POUNDS OF ALMOST 24 KARAT GOLD TREASURE.

Salvaging continues to this day and the man who put the "treasure" back into treasure hunting, Mel Fisher, has expanded his operations.

1986

On May 13, the GSA decides to put Truman Annex (see 1975) on the auction block. The bidding will be held on September 10, 1986.

By August 29, the auction had generated over 300 inquiries including one from Alaskan Indians holding bazillions of federal land credit dollars.

On the morning of September 10, over 500 people crowd into Jan McArt's Cabaret Theatre at Mallory Square. The auction for Truman Annex comprising 43 acres of prime waterfront territory including Truman's Little White House, the 27-acre Tank Island and 32 acres of submerged bay bottom begins.

The bidding runs right up to $17,000,000 -- led by the Alaskan Indians and Pritam Singh, who is fashionably garbed in dungarees, hiking boots and blue turban. Singh raises the bid to $17,250,000 and the hammer falls.

Singh announces plans, via his new Truman Annex Company, to develop waterfront hotels, luxury housing, condos, a marina and yacht club, shops, boardwalk, affordable housing, the restoration of the Little White House on the Annex and creation of a tropical lagooned paradise on Tank Island.

1987

Pahe'e, the sealion, escapes and abandons pregnant wife Lani. Conch wood carver Mario Sanchez visits from Tampa and once again sets up his "studio under the trees." Mel Fisher discovers more treasure and then finds submerged Navy 'Avenger' aircraft near the Dry Tortugas ... "Bermuda Triangle" aficionados perk up. Hurricane Floyd and the *Islip Garbage Barge* visit Key West. Pritam Singh sets up a roadblock on the road (his) into the Post Office; Postal Authorities find time to negotiate easement rights; Conch Republic officials designate Singh as Postmaster General. Amy DePoo, Richard Heyman, Sonny McCoy, Captain Tony and Love 22 run for Mayor; Heyman wins.

One of Key West's great people, Heavy Duty, passes away. Heavy grew up on the sea, hung out with the Huttons on Long Island, bought an airplane and enjoyed a notoriously short history as a self-taught pilot, was a commercial fisherman and vegetable tycoon, ate his shrimp raw, was 'just about' opinionated and was buried at sea. His picture hangs at the Full Moon Saloon.

1988

Key West again moves into another transitional period that features the highest cost of living (for locals and tourists) in the State of Florida; hotel, resort and supporting business construction soars as a crisis looms on where the service personnel will be able to afford to live; U.S. Secretary of the Interior Donald Hodel has called for off-shore drilling within 25 miles of Key West.

Russell Keene initiates the first Key West-to-satellite uplink regularly scheduled TV series.

The Navy announces plans to construct military housing at Peary Court, a 29 acre park the City has under lease expiring 3/90. The grounds harbor city softball fields, scruffy green spaces, some trees and a bank.

"License to Kill," a new James Bond movie, is filmed in town and up the Keys; Don Johnson wins the $1,000,000 Key West Offshore Cup Boat Race.

Former Key West Mayor C.B. Harvey passes on. He is survived by wife Wilhelmina "Wild Willy" Harvey, First Woman Mayor of the Fabulous Florida Keys. It seems that, while cruising Duval (without permission) during her reckless youth, she spied her father driving directly towards her. With great and panicking teenage wisdom, she ducked down behind her steering wheel and then proceeded to involve herself in a head on collision with Dad.

1989

First Federal Savings and Loan of the Florida Keys goes belly up $45,000,000+ in the hole, taken over by the Resolution Trust Corp. and sold to Barnett Bank.

In June, thousands of locals protest against potential oil drilling off the Keys. Black flags fly, Interior Secretary Manuel Lujan and Florida Governor Lawton Chiles, who is big time against it, visit to see if there <u>could be(?)</u> any possible environmental impact.

June 1990: President Bush bans oil drilling off the Keys until at least 2000.

WORLD FAMOUS "WILLOUGHBY THE CAT" HEDGING ON POSITION DURING MAYORAL CAMPAIGN

Mayoral results: Perennial candidate and bar owner Capt. Tony Tarracino defeats Tom Sawyer 3,049 to 3,017. "Willoughby the Cat" garners 37 official write-in, but not officially counted, votes. Tony wins by a whisker.

1990

"Winston the Horse" is surprise-attacked on his "dangles' by ("Unknown the Pit Bull"), seeks refuge on top of a car, thus ending the short lived era of horse drawn carriages in Old Town.

VIEW OF THE OLD ARMORY ON WHITE STREET FROM PEARY COURT IN PARK STATUS.

Protesters and petitioners scramble around town concerning Peary Court (see 1988). In June, after presented with a keep-it-a-local-park-status petition of over 5,000 names, the Navy announces 160 homes to be built. Alarms go into overdrive concerning the lack of historic esthetics and impact studies of the planned community.

Peary Court started in the 1830's as military barracks, cemetery and parade grounds and was torn down (more like swept up) in the 1950's to make way for spiffy looking CBS (cement block structure) project "bungalows" constructed for Navy housing. That development closed in the 1970's, was leveled and rented to the City for $1.00 a year for use as a park until March, 1990.

In November, the softball fields are demolished, the grounds are leveled and Capt. Jack Ensch orders the park to be secured by Navy personnel. On 12/4 Molly Logan chains herself to a ficus tree on the property and pretty much sets up treehouse-keeping on a platform constructed earlier on ... she's removed and arrested 5 days later (acquitted 6/30/91).

A big bunch of official hoopla involving everybody erupts: the City Commission has resolutions for and against ... and then, on 1/13/94, former City Commissioner Harry Powell, adamant foe of the project, holes up in a construction trailer with a petrol/fertilizer bomb for several hours before surrendering (guilty 5/6/94 ... he serves a year).

Peary Court opens 4/20/1995. Navy announces during the summer of 1995 that $800,000 has been budgeted to upgrade kitchen cabinets.

1991

State closes Berenson's Key West Greyhound Track citing charges of illegal sewers and animal cruelty. The track site has been suggested for a new County Jail, which was later built waterfront at a cost of $30 million beside Mt. Trashmore, the local dump, which is now capped.

A Cuban pilot defects in a MIG and lands aircraft at Boca Chica Naval Air Station. Here's the cool part: although undetected by NAS, the MIG, as it circles Key West 3 times at 100' altitude, is bogeyed by Freddy Cabanas while flying in his biplane and escorted to landing. During September, 1993, a second MIG drops in!

City announces referendum to buy Singleton Property, rustic old shrimper territory waterfront at the Historic Key West Bight. The property is 8.5 acres along Caroline Street.

Man throws rattlesnake on cheating wife and partner while they're in bed.

1992

As economic conditions deteriorate in Cuba, spring tides and breezes bring a considerably larger exodus of Cuban rafters than in recent years. By the end of the year, the number passes more than 2,500. 1993 yields over 3,600. In June, 1994, the numbers threaten to more than quadruple (8/20/94 USCG rescues over 3,000) and US President Clinton announces policy to quarantine all refugees at Guantanamo Bay, Cuba, which by September houses over 15,000.

August 24: Hurricane Andrew destroys Homestead on the mainland and in the process also kills electric and phones in Key West. As there is no communication with Key West, CNN announces that we've probably been destroyed. In reality, winds and rain and damage are minimal down here.

1993

After a successful referendum, City closes deal to buy Key West Bight for $18.5 million. Featuring the old romantic shrimp boatin' days of old, the Bight is to be carefully preserved from unsympathetic, tacky, commercial development. The first presented plans feature an asphalt parking lot and a little old family restaurant called "Hooters." Back to the drawing board. "B.O.'s Fish Wagon" announces plans to abandon Duval St. and move to anchor Bight corner of William and Caroline.

"KEY WEST TV SERIES": A really hilarious Fox comedy TV series about those wacky, colorful characters of Key West. Premiers 10/92; not one Key Wester will admit to watching an entire episode (only the part "I" was in, the rest stinks), dismal failure rating's wise and canceled 2/93.

KEY WEST CITIZEN

CRIME REPORT

Police: Someone stole man's in-ground pool

Police: Man threw eggs, china over balcony

Adjusting to the pressures of paradise, locals scan the "Key West Citizen Crime Reports" to see what the neighbors are up to. The all-time faxed around the world headline appears 6/22/93: 'Man Allegedly Bites Roommate In Crotch'... stitches for a 4-inch gash ... YEOWTCH!! Runnerups (it's an honor just to be nominated) include the coroner's report of a suicide involving a fellow fished from the channel with feet cured in concrete, arms tied by wire; Mrs. Weaver, who after blasting Mr. 'Sizzling' Weaver with 7 rounds and reloading quotes: "Now you're really gonna git it ..." BANG ... BANG ... BANG ... BANG! (not guilty); 'Rocky the Chihuahua' being sued for impregnating a purebred Rottweiler; a man stepping over a dead body for 3 weeks 'cause he thought the deceased was being ornery; two guys after a multiple rolling of their BMW on U.S. 1 only to land wheels down and then continue driving on: when stopped (roof crushed/back window shattered) explain that they thought the wreck had been a hallucination; main power lines cut up the Keys (1995!) for a burglary and 'Chi Chi' the pot belly pig charged with sexually assaulting and causing fender damage to a parked Harley (sentence: "CASTRATION" because that's the rules!!!). Sometimes Key West is called 'Bellevue with a Liquor License.'

1994

"It looks like some kind of third world outpost!" Dedicated July 4, 1956, the Key West International Airport terminal has since grown with the addition of several desks and chairs and stuff while air traffic has increased well over 1000%. Talks begin to explore joint usage with the Naval Air Station at Boca Chica which, of course, bog down.

Time for a new airport terminal. The first new design meets with howls of "It looks like somethin' out o' Boca Raytone!" Six more designs are presented for a public vote with a Conch style job winning handily. More discussion, still bogged down, except now you have to pay for parking.

1994

S.S. SUNWARD DOCKS AT MALLORY SQUARE 9/70 INITIATING THE AGE OF CRUISE SHIPS.
UP UNTIL THIS PERIOD, SHIPS WERE PRETTY MUCH IN YOUR BASIC TRANSPORTATION CATEGORY,
IN THAT THEY WERE ON THEIR WAY SOMEWHERE.

Cruise ship statistics for 1994:
    Number of visits; 368
    Passenger count: 398,370
    City revenues from docking charges: $852,887

Other local facts for 1994:
    Key West human population: 26,417
    Per capita personal income: $22,056
    Rank of cost of living in Florida: #1
    Number of guest rooms: 4,753
    Number of guests: 2,000,000+
    Number of restaurants: 283 and all of 'em that don't have a
        drive-thru serve fresh seafood.
    Key West chicken population: couple of million; some of whom
        have exhibited gravity-defying, low level flying/swooping talents
        (it appears to the viewer as a cannonball heading at a leisurely
        pace, right towards you).

June 7, 1994

Key West Shipwreck Historeum
brings back to life Master Wrecker
Asa Tift with live actors, video
displays, laser technology and
artifacts. It was shipwrecking that
made Key West the richest city in
the mid 1800's and today can be
relived at this one-of-a-kind
attraction.

KEY WEST SHIPWRECK HISTOREUM.

BIG FIRE: EARLY 8/4/95, KEY WEST HAS ITS BIGGEST FIRE IN 70 YEARS AS HALF OF THE 600 BLOCK OF DUVAL STREET (INCLUDING ANTONIA'S [SEE PHOTOS 1975] AND THE COPA) BURNS TO THE GROUND. THE FIRE WAS DELIBERATELY SET. THE KEY WEST FIRE DEPARTMENT PERFORMS A FANTASTIC JOB OF CONTROLLING THE SPREAD OF THE BLAZE; SIMILAR FIRES HAVE DESTROYED ENTIRE DISTRICTS. NEW CONSTRUCTION BEGINS IMMEDIATELY TO MOVE THROUGH THE "PROCESS."

1995

The only coral reef in North America, 7 miles off Key West, shows signs of serious deterioration caused by toxic runoff from mainland farms, injection wells and diverted Everglades fresh water flow.

Key West High School (35-2) wins its 8th State 4A baseball championship and is ranked #2 nationally by Collegiate Baseball America. The athletic department places over 30 scholarships per year and is pursuing an aggressive priority in female sports.

Mel Fisher (see 1985) dreams of the location of more *Atocha* treasure; the real BIG motherlode stored in the ship's stern where the rich folks bunked.

The ocean is still tourmaline aqua and loaded with more colour than a crystal; Key West has the best behaved dogs in the country; bicycle riding is a joyous necessity; the fishing is a surefire hit and the weather is just fine.

- - - - - to be continued - - - - -

1997

After two years of hard work and planning, the Key West Historical Memorial Sculpture Garden opens in a former vacant lot. The garden, located in the heart of Mallory Square, features the busts and biographies of 36 of the island's most influential people. A magnificent centerpiece depicts the wreckers salvaging a ship that has come the ultimate peril over the reef. A weekend long celebration ensues event with a hurricane- like storm canceling many of the festivities.

KEY WEST HISTORIAL MEMORIAL SCULPTURE GARDEN

Cayo Hueso y Habana HISTOREUM®, a Cuban themed emporium, opens in the historic Mallory Square area in September. Housed in a historic brick warehouse built by William Wall in 1879, the HISTOREUM® focuses on Key West's connection with Cuba through photographs, displays, artwork by acclaimed artist Mario Sanchez, a cigar shop, and Cuban restaurant.

CAYO HUESO Y HABANA HISTOREUM®

1998

The last working schooner ever built in the United States, the *Western Union*, returns to Key West. Built in 1939 by Thompson Enterprises and leased to the Western Union Telegraph Company, the schooner was built and used to lay undersea telegraph cable throughout the Caribbean. Today it sails twice a day giving guests a glimpse of Key West's maritime past. The *Western Union* is the flagship of city of Key West and is listed on the National Register of Historic Places.

SCHOONER WESTERN UNION

September 25, 1998. Hurricane Georges pays a visit to Key West and the Florida Keys. Georges is the first hurricane to directly affect Key West since 1987 and only the second one since 1966. Estimated winds speeds at Key West Airport were from 69 to 87 mph., with the center of the storm in the lower Keys. The highest winds, though, could not be recorded as the airport lost power. While no deaths were reported, 173 houses were destroyed, there was major damage to 147 homes, including 75 houseboats. Damage was estimated at $250 million dollars, with extensive damage to the loose rooted ficus trees around the island. Power outages lasted upwards of two weeks, forcing neighbors to rely on each other, rather then their TV's, radios, and VCRS for entertainment. Officials close city off to tourism. On October 4, Key West re-opens for tourism four days sooner than expected .

DAMAGE OF HURRICANE GEORGES

Treasure salvor Mel Fisher dies after a lengthy battle with cancer in December, 1998.

1999

Key West elects a new mayor, Jimmy Weekley, a 14 year veteran city commissioner. Weekley captures 59% of the vote defeating incumbent mayor Sheila Mullins.

Hurricane Irene sweeps across Key West on October 14 with maximum winds at 75mph and 12 inches of rain. New mayor Jimmy Weekley said, "This was a lamb compared to the last one."

2000

Flagler Station Over-sea Railway HISTOREUM® Museum opens on the site of the old Margaret Street spur of the Florida East Coast Railway. This HISTOREUM® is a museum and tribute to Henry Flagler's engineering miracle, the Key West Extension the Florida East Coast Railroad, which was built and ran 130 miles out to sea.

FLAGLER STATION OVER-SEA RAILWAY HISTOREUM®

KEY WEST HOME GROWN BUSINESSES

OLD TOWN TROLLEY TOURS NATIONAL HEADQUARTERS
P.O. Box 1237, Key West, FL 33041 - (305) 296-6688
The Old Town Trolley has operated its continuously loop tours in
Key West since 1980. With 14 stops, guests can disembark to shop,
dine and visit attractions. Old Town Trolley Tours can also be
found in Boston, Cambridge, San Diego, Savannah and Washington.

KEY WEST AQUARIUM
#1 Whitehead St., Key West, FL 33040 - (305) 296-2051
Constructed in 1934, the "Aquarium" presents an excellent display
of Key West's tremendous variety of sea life with special attractions
made possible by our close proximity to North America's only living

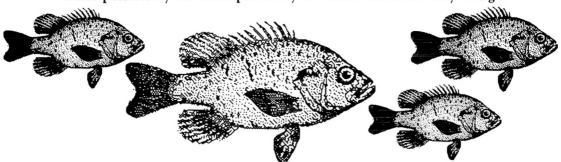

coral reef. The facility is located at harbor's edge and features
tropical fish, touch tank, Atlantic Shore exhibit, turtles ... and sharks!
The staff takes seriously its responsibility to protect the marine
environment and provide an informative learning experience for all ages.

KEY WEST HAND PRINT FABRICS AND FASHION
201 Simonton St., Key West, FL 33040 - (305) 294-9535
When first opened in 1961, "Handprint" surged to the fashion
storefronts with gaily designed and locally inspired tropical patterns.
Under the direction of Lily Pulitzer the designs matured to the
covers of "Vogue." Today you are invited to their enormous
(considering Key West) studio for an informative, colorful and
unique shopping experience of an integral part of Key West's
social history.

KEY WEST SPONGE MARKET
#1 Whitehead St., Key West, FL 33040 - (305) 294-2555
It's a fact! The world's finest sponges come from Key West waters
and the Sponge Market is carefully developing an historic and
environmentally sensitive re-emergence of the industry. Local
spongers, still working with hooks, harvest several varieties of
natural sponges which are then processed and sold at the Sponge
Market or shipped to international distributors. Be sure and catch
C.B. McHugh, the "King of the Spongers" in his documentary
sponging video playing non-stop at the Sponge Market.

WORLD FAMOUS CONCH TOUR TRAIN
501 Front Street, Key West, FL 33040 - (305) 294-5161
One of Florida's most popular attractions, the Conch Tour Train
has been entertaining visitors to Key West since 1958. Tours
depart daily from the heart of Old Town Key West.

BIBLIOGRAPHY

Artman, L.P. Jr. "KEY WEST HISTORY"
    Key West: L.P. Artman, 1969
Brothers, Betty. "WRECKERS AND WORKERS OF OLD
    KEY WEST"
    Big Pine Key: Litoky, 1972
Browne, Jefferson B. "KEY WEST HISTORY, THE OLD
    AND THE NEW"
    Tallahassee: Bicentennial Commission of Florida, 1973
"BIRDS EYE VIEW OF KEY WEST"
    Madison, Wisconsin: C.S. Moore Company, 1884
Carter, Samuel III. "THE GULF STREAM STORY"
    Garden City, New York: Doubleday & Company, Inc., 1970
Kaufelt, Lynn Mitsuko. "KEY WEST WRITERS AND
    THEIR HOUSES"
    Englewood, Florida: Pineapple Press, 1986
Langley, Joan and Wright. "KEY WEST IMAGES OF THE PAST"
    Key West: Key West Images of the Past, Inc., 1982
Maloney, Walter C. "A SKETCH OF THE HISTORY OF
    KEY WEST, FLORIDA"
    Floridiana Facsimile & Reprint Series
    Gainsville: University of Florida Press, 1876
Parks, Pat. "THE RAILROAD THAT DIED AT SEA"
    Key West: The Langely Press, 1968
Smith, Wayne S. "THE CLOSEST OF ENEMIES"
    New York: W.W. Norton & Co., 1987
Wells, Sharon. "SOLARES HILL WALKING AND BIKING GUIDE"
    Key West: Solares Hill Co., 1986
Windhorn, Stan and Wright Langley. "YESTERDAY'S FLORIDA
    KEYS"
    Key West: The Langley Press Inc., 1974
Windhorn, Stan and Wright Langley. "YESTERDAY'S KEY WEST"
    Key West: The Langley Press, Inc., 1973

NEWSPAPER

"KEY WEST CITIZEN," 1950 - 1987

TELEVISION

"ATOCHA: QUEST FOR TREASURE"
    Produced by Tom Simon, Written by Nancy LeBrun
    A National Geographic EXPLORER Production, 1986
"THE STORY OF OLD CITY HALL, KEY WEST"
    Produced the The Historic Florida Keys Preservation Board,
    Written by Stephen Nichols
    An F.I.U. Board of Regents Production, 1987

RESOURCES

MONROE COUNTY MAY HILL RUSSELL LIBRARY
    700 Fleming St., Key West, FL 33040 (305) 294-8488
    The Florida History Department covers local, state and
    Caribbean history as well as architecture, natural history,
    economics, genealogy and geography. The best part is the staff
    who operate with a scholarly, hometown and pleasant
    attitude. We urge you to use and support your local libraries.